CW00506859

365 WISDOMS OF THE PROPHET MUHAMMAD

Authentic Texts from the Hadith and Sunnah
on the Family, Health, Success and Spiritual
Growth (Collection - Islamic Books)

IBRAHIM AL-ABADI & ISLAM WAY

ORIGINAL VERSION

ALL RIGHTS RESERVED, IN PARTICULAR WITH REGARD TO THE USE AND DISTRIBUTION OF TEXTS, TABLES AND GRAPHICS.

COPYRIGHT © 2024 BOOK SHELTER GMBH

ISBN: 978-3-98929-068-6

LEGAL NOTICE:

BOOK SHELTER GMBH
AUFHÄUSERSTRASSE 64
30457 HANNOVER
GERMANY

THIS BOOK IS FOR

FROM

TABLE OF CONTENTS

FOREWORD

Assalamu Alaykum,

Thank you for holding in your hands this book with 365 words of wisdom from our Prophet Muhammad (ﷺ) and for wanting to be closer to Allah (ﷻ), our Creator.

The wisdom shared in this book is derived from the hadith and sunnah, organized into relevant aspects of life. You will discover hadiths covering true faith in Allah (ﷻ), proper conduct towards people and animals, considerations for personal and family well-being, guidance on protection and support, and much more.

Hadiths are traditions of what the Prophet Muhammad (ﷺ) said, did or (silently) accepted. After the Holy Qur'an, these traditions are the second most important source of Islam. Not only do they give us an insight into the life of the time, but they also enable us to understand important pillars of the Islamic faith. We can also benefit from Muhammad (ﷺ) numerous words of wisdom and draw valuable conclusions for leading a happy and fulfilled life as a Muslim.

In addition to the original Arabic text and source, in this book you will find a careful English translation of all the hadiths.

Ibrahim Al-Abadi and Islam Way hope you enjoy reading the wisdom of our Prophet ﷺ.

عظم الله اجركم

Let us start, with the blessing of Allah.

HADITHS ON TRUE FAITH

عَنِ النَّبِيِّ صَلَّى اللَّهُ عَلَيْهِ وَسَلَّمَ قَالَ " الْمُسْلِمُ مَنْ سَلِمَ الْمُسْلِمُونَ مِنْ لِسَانِهِ وَيَدِهِ، وَالْمُهَاجِرُ مَنْ هَجَرَ مَا نَهَى اللَّهُ عَنْهُ ".

The Prophet (ﷺ) said, "A Muslim is one who avoids hurting Muslims with his tongue and his hands. And a muhajir (emigrant) is one who renounces all that Allah has forbidden."

Sahih Al-Bukhari, hadith number 10

ـ قَالَ رَسُولُ اللَّهِ صَلَّى اللَّهُ عَلَيْهِ وَسَلَّمَ " يَأْتِي الشَّيْطَانُ أَحَدَكُمْ فَيَقُولُ مَنْ خَلَقَ كَذَا مَنْ خَلَقَ كَذَا حَتَّى يَقُولَ مَنْ خَلَقَ رَبَّكَ فَإِذَا بَلَغَهُ فَلْيَسْتَعِذْ بِاللَّهِ، وَلْيَنْتَهِ ".

The Messenger of Allah (ﷺ) said, "Satan comes to one of you and says, "Who created so-and-so?" until he says, "Who created your Lord?" So, when he asks such a question, one should take refuge in Allah and abandon such thoughts."

Sahih Al-Bukhari, hadith number 3276

قَالَ رَسُولُ اللَّهِ صَلَّى اللَّهُ عَلَيْهِ وَسَلَّمَ " الْمُسْلِمُ مَنْ سَلِمَ النَّاسُ مِنْ لِسَانِهِ وَيَدِهِ وَالْمُؤْمِنُ مَنْ أَمِنَهُ النَّاسُ عَلَى دِمَائِهِمْ وَأَمْوَالِهِمْ ".

The Messenger of Allah (ﷺ) said, "The Muslim is the one from whose tongue and hands people are safe, and the believer is the one from whose life and wealth people are safe."

Sunan Al-Nasa'i, hadith number 4995

HADITHS ON TRUE FAITH

عَنْ رَسُولِ اللهِ صَلَّى اللهُ عَلَيْهِ وَسَلَّمَ أنه قال: " الرُّوْيَا الصَّالِحَةُ جُزْءٌ مِنْ سِتَّةٍ وَأَرْبَعِينَ جُزْءًا مِنْ النُّبْوَةِ ".

The Prophet (ﷺ) said, "The (good) dreams of a faithful believer are part of the forty-six parts of prophecy."

Sahih Al-Bukhari, hadith number 6987

كَانَ رَسُولُ اللهِ صلى الله عليه وسلم إِذَا قَامَ مِنَ اللَّيْلِ (للصلاة) يَشُوصُ فَاهُ بِالسِّوَاكِ.

When the Messenger of Allah (ﷺ) would get up at night (for prayer), he would wipe his mouth with a toothpick.

Sunan Abu Dawûd, hadith number 55

قَالَ رَسُولُ اللهِ صَلَّى اللهُ عَلَيْهِ وَسَلَّمَ " إِذَا جَاءَ رَمَضَانُ فُتِحَتْ أَبْوَابُ الْجَنَّةِ ".

The Messenger of Allah (ﷺ) said, "When Ramadan begins, the gates of Paradise are wide open."

Sahih Al-Bukhari, hadith number 1898

HADITHS ON TRUE FAITH

قَالَ رَسُولُ اللهِ صَلَّى اللهُ عَلَيْهِ وَسَلَّمَ " إِذَا جَاءَ أَحَدُكُمُ الْجُمُعَةَ فَلْيَغْتَسِلْ ".

The Messenger of Allah (ﷺ) said, "When Friday
comes, you should take a bath before going
to the mosque for the Friday prayer."

Sahih Al-Bukhari, hadith number 877

قَالَ رَسُولُ اللهِ صَلَّى اللهُ عَلَيْهِ وَسَلَّمَ " أَلاَ أُخْبِرُكُمْ بِأَكْبَرِ الْكَبَائِرِ ". قَالُوا
بَلَى يَا رَسُولَ اللهِ. قَالَ " الإِشْرَاكُ بِاللهِ، وَعُقُوقُ الْوَالِدَيْنِ ".

The Messenger of Allah (ﷺ) said, "Would you like me to
inform you of the greatest of sins?" They said, "Yes, O
Messenger of Allah (ﷺ)!" He said, "Worshipping Allah
together with another diety and disobeying one's parents."

Sahih Al-Bukhari, hadith number 6273

قَالَ رَسُولُ اللهِ صَلَّى اللهُ عَلَيْهِ وَسَلَّمَ "خيركم من تعلم القرآن وعلمه".

The Messenger of Allah (ﷺ) said, "The best among you
is the one who learns the Qur'an and teaches it."

Riyad as-Salihin, hadith number 993

HADITHS ON TRUE FAITH

قَالَ رَسُولُ اللهِ صَلَّى اللهُ عَلَيْهِ وَسَلَّمَ " الدُّنْيَا سِجْنُ الْمُؤْمِنِ وَجَنَّةُ الْكَافِرِ ".

The Messenger of Allah (ﷺ) said, "The world is a prison for the believer and a paradise for the disbeliever."

Sahih Muslim, hadith number 2956

عَنِ النَّبِيِّ صَلَّى اللهُ عَلَيْهِ وَسَلَّمَ قَالَ " يَقْبِضُ اللهُ الْأَرْضَ يَوْمَ الْقِيَامَةِ، وَيَطْوِي السَّمَاءَ بِيَمِينِهِ ثُمَّ يَقُولُ أَنَا الْمَلِكُ أَيْنَ مُلُوكُ الْأَرْضِ؟".

The Prophet (ﷺ) said, "On the Day of Resurrection, Allah will uphold the whole earth and bend the sky with His right hand and say, "I am the King, where are the kings of the earth?""

Sahih Al-Bukhari, hadith number 7382

عن سهل بن سعد قال: " كُنتُ أَتَسَحَّرُ في أَهْلي، ثُمَّ تَكُونُ سُرْعَتي أَنْ أُدْرِكَ السُّجُودَ مع رَسُولِ اللهِ صَلَّى اللهُ عليه وسلَّمَ [...]."

Sahl bin Saad related, "I used to take my Suhur meals with my family and then rush for Fajr prayer with the Prophet (ﷺ) [...]."

Sahih Al-Bukhari, hadith number 1920

HADITHS ON TRUE FAITH

قَالَ النَّبِيُّ صلى الله عليه وسلم " مَنْ رَآنِي فِي الْمَنَامِ فَقَدْ رَآنِي، فَإِنَّ الشَّيْطَانَ لاَ يَتَخَيَّلُ بِي ".

The Prophet (ﷺ) said, "Whoever has seen me in his dreams has certainly seen me, for Satan cannot take on my appearance."

Sahih Al-Bukhari, hadith number 6994

قَالَ النَّبِيُّ صلى الله عليه وسلم " مَنْ قَاتَلَ لِتَكُونَ كَلِمَةُ اللَّهِ (الإسلام) هِيَ الْعُلْيَا فَهُوَ فِي سَبِيلِ اللَّهِ عَزَّ وَجَلَّ ".

The Prophet (ﷺ) said, "Whoever fights to make the word of Allah (Islam) predominant, fights for the cause of Allah, Almighty and Exalted."

Sahih Al-Bukhari, hadith number 123

قَالَ رَسُولُ اللهِ صَلَّى اللهُ عَلَيْهِ وَسَلَّمَ: " لَنْ يَشْبَعَ الْمُؤْمِنُ مِنْ خَيْرٍ يَسْمَعُهُ حَتَّى يَكُونَ مُنْتَهَاهُ الْجَنَّةَ."

The Messenger of Allah (ﷺ) said, "A believer will never be satisfied with the good he hears until he reaches Paradise."

Mishkát al-Masabíh, hadith number 222

HADITHS ON TRUE FAITH

قَالَ رَسُولُ اللهِ صَلَّى اللهُ عَلَيْهِ وَسَلَّمَ: " إِذَا جَاءَ رَمَضَانُ فُتِّحَتْ أَبْوَابُ الْجَنَّةِ وَغُلِّقَتْ أَبْوَابُ النَّارِ وَصُفِّدَتِ الشَّيَاطِينُ".

The Messenger of Allah (ﷺ) said, "When the month of Ramadan comes, the gates of Paradise are widely opened and the gates of Hell are firmly closed and the devils are chained."

Sahih Muslim, hadith number 1079a

قَالَ رَسُولُ اللهِ صَلَّى اللهُ عَلَيْهِ وَسَلَّمَ: " من كان يؤمن بالله واليوم الآخر، فليقل خيرًا، أو ليصمت ".

The Prophet (ﷺ) said, "Whoever believes in Allah and the Day of Resurrection should say good things or remain silent."

Riyad as-Salihin, hadith number 1511

كَانَ النَّبِيُّ صَلَّى اللهُ عَلَيْهِ وَسَلَّمَ لَيَقُومُ لِيُصَلِّيَ حَتَّى تَرِمُ قَدَمَاهُ أَوْ سَاقَاهُ, فَيُقَالُ لَهُ: فَيَقُولُ: " أَفَلَا أَكُونُ عَبْدًا شَكُورًا ".

The Prophet (ﷺ) used to stand to pray at night until both his feet or legs swelled. He was asked why and he replied, "Shouldn't I be a grateful servant?".

Sahih Al-Bukhari, hadith number 1130

HADITHS ON TRUE FAITH

قَالَ رَسُولُ اللهِ صَلَّى اللهُ عَلَيْهِ وَسَلَّمَ " مِفْتَاحُ الصَّلَاةِ الطُّهُورُ وَتَحْرِيمُهَا التَّكْبِيرُ وَتَحْلِيلُهَا التَّسْلِيمُ " .

The Messenger of Allah (ﷺ) said, "The key of prayer is ablution purification; its opening is takbir and its end is taslim."

Sunan Abu Dawûd, hadith number 61

عَنِ الأَشْعَثِ قَالَ " إِذَا سَمِعَ ﷺ الصَّارِخَ قَامَ فَصَلَّى".

Al-Ash'az related, "The Prophet (ﷺ) got up to pray when he heard the crowing of a rooster."

Sahih Al-Bukhari, hadith number 1132b

عَنْ عَبْدِ اللهِ ـ رضى الله عنه ـ قَالَ ذُكِرَ عِنْدَ النَّبِيِّ صَلَّى اللهُ عَلَيْهِ وَسَلَّمَ رَجُلٌ فَقِيلَ مَا زَالَ نَائِمًا حَتَّى أَصْبَحَ مَا قَامَ إِلَى الصَّلَاةِ. فَقَالَ " بَالَ الشَّيْطَانُ فِي أُذُنِهِ ".

Abdullah (may Allah be pleased with him) related, "A person was mentioned to the Prophet(ﷺ) and was told that he had slept until morning and did not get up for prayer. The Prophet (ﷺ) said, 'Satan urinated in his ears.'"

Sahih Al-Bukhari, hadith number 1144

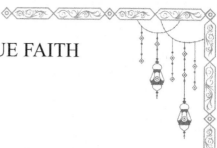

HADITHS ON TRUE FAITH

قَالَ رَسُولُ اللَّهِ صَلَّى اللَّهُ عَلَيْهِ وَسَلَّمَ: "مَنْ يُرِدِ اللَّهُ بِهِ خَيْرًا يُفَقِّهْهُ فِي الدِّينِ."

The Messenger of Allah (ﷺ) said, "When Allah wishes good for someone, He gives him deep understanding of religion."

Riyad as-Salihin, hadith number 1376

[...] سَمِعْتُ رَسُولَ اللَّهِ صَلَّى اللَّهُ عَلَيْهِ وَسَلَّمَ قَالَ " مَنْ رَأَى مُنْكَرًا فَلْيُغَيِّرْهُ بِيَدِهِ فَإِنْ لَمْ يَسْتَطِعْ فَبِلِسَانِهِ فَإِنْ لَمْ يَسْتَطِعْ فَبِقَلْبِهِ وَذَلِكَ أَضْعَفُ الْإِيمَانِ ".

[...] "I heard Allah's Messenger (ﷺ) say: 'Whoever among you sees an evil thing, let him change it with his hand; if he cannot, let him do it with his tongue; if he cannot, let him do it with his heart; and that is the weakest form of faith.'"

Sunan Al Nasa'i, hadith number 5008

قَالَ النَّبِيُّ صَلَّى اللَّهُ عَلَيْهِ وَسَلَّمَ " تَسَحَّرُوا فَإِنَّ فِي السَّحُورِ بَرَكَةً ".

The Prophet (ﷺ) said, "Eat the Suhur (pre-dawn meal), for therein lies a blessing."

Sahih Al-Bukhari, hadith number 1923

HADITHS ON TRUE FAITH

قَالَ رَسُولُ اللهِ ـ صَلَّى اللهُ عَلَيْهِ وَسَلَّمَ ـ " ذَرُونِي مَا تَرَكْتُكُمْ فَإِنَّمَا هَلَكَ مَنْ كَانَ قَبْلَكُمْ بِسُؤَالِهِمْ وَاخْتِلَافِهِمْ عَلَى أَنْبِيَائِهِمْ فَإِذَا أَمَرْتُكُمْ بِشَيْءٍ فَخُذُوا مِنْهُ مَا اسْتَطَعْتُمْ وَإِذَا نَهَيْتُكُمْ عَنْ شَيْءٍ فَانْتَهُوا".

The Messenger of Allah (ﷺ) said, "Be satisfied with what I have left you therefore. For those who came before you perished because of their many questions and disagreements with their prophets. If I have commanded you to do something, do it to the best of your ability. And if I have forbidden you to do anything, do not do it".

Sunan Ibn Mayah, hadith number 2

قَالَ رَسُولُ اللهِ صَلَّى اللهُ عَلَيْهِ وَسَلَّمَ " ثَلَاثَةٌ لَهُمْ أَجْرَانِ رَجُلٌ مِنْ أَهْلِ الْكِتَابِ آمَنَ بِنَبِيِّهِ، وَآمَنَ بِمُحَمَّدٍ صلى الله عليه وسلم وَالْعَبْدُ الْمَمْلُوكُ إِذَا أَدَّى حَقَّ اللهِ وَحَقَّ مَوَالِيهِ، وَرَجُلٌ كَانَتْ عِنْدَهُ أَمَةٌ {يَطُؤُهَا} فَأَدَّبَهَا، فَأَحْسَنَ تَأْدِيبَهَا، وَعَلَّمَهَا فَأَحْسَنَ تَعْلِيمَهَا، ثُمَّ أَعْتَقَهَا فَتَزَوَّجَهَا، فَلَهُ أَجْرَانِ ".

The Messenger of Allah (ﷺ) said, "Three people will receive double reward:1. a jew or a Christian who believed in their Prophet (Jesus or Moses) and then believed in the Prophet (ﷺ) Muhammad (i.e. embraced Islam). 2. a servant who fulfills his duties towards Allah and his lord 3. a master of a female servant who teaches her good manners and educates her in the best possible way (religion), sets her free and then marries her."

Sahih Al-Bukhari, hadith number 97

HADITHS ON TRUE FAITH

قَالَ رَسُولُ اللهِ صَلَّى اللهُم عَلَيْهِ وَسَلَّمَ: "إِنَّ اللهَ قَالَ مَنْ عَادَى لِي وَلِيًّا فَقَدْ آذَنْتُهُ بِالْحَرْبِ وَمَا تَقَرَّبَ إِلَيَّ عَبْدِي بِشَيْءٍ أَحَبَّ إِلَيَّ مِمَّا افْتَرَضْتُ عَلَيْهِ وَمَا يَزَالُ عَبْدِي يَتَقَرَّبُ إِلَيَّ بِالنَّوَافِلِ حَتَّى أُحِبَّهُ فَإِذَا أَحْبَبْتُهُ كُنْتُ سَمْعَهُ الَّذِي يَسْمَعُ بِهِ وَبَصَرَهُ الَّذِي يُبْصِرُ بِهِ وَيَدَهُ الَّتِي يَبْطِشُ بِهَا وَرِجْلَهُ الَّتِي يَمْشِي بِهَا وَإِنْ سَأَلَنِي لَأُعْطِيَنَّهُ وَلَئِنْ اسْتَعَاذَنِي لَأُعِيذَنَّهُ [...]".

The Messenger of Allah (ﷺ) said, "Allah says: 'Whosoever is hostile to one of My pious servants, I will declare war on him. My servant does not approach Me with anything dearer to Me than the duties I have imposed upon him. And by the performance of voluntary acts of worship, he draws nearer and nearer to Me until I love him. When I love him, I am his ear by which he hears, his eye by which he sees, his hand by which he grasps, and his foot by which he walks. If he asks anything of Me, I give it to him, and if he seeks refuge in Me, I would surely grant him refuge [...]"

Riyad as-Salihin, hadith number 95

قَالَ رَسُولُ اللهِ صَلَّى اللهُ عَلَيْهِ وَسَلَّمَ "الإِيمَانُ بِضْعٌ وَسَبْعُونَ شُعْبَةً وَالْحَيَاءُ شُعْبَةٌ مِنَ الإِيمَانِ".

The Messenger of Allah (ﷺ) said, "Faith consists of seventy parts, and modesty is one of them."

Sunan Al Nasa'i, hadith number 5004

قَالَ رَسُولُ اللهِ صَلَّى اللهُ عَلَيْهِ وَسَلَّمَ "خيرُكم مَن تعلَّمَ القرآنَ وعلَّمَهُ".

The Messenger of Allah (ﷺ) said, "The best of you is the one who learns and teaches the Qur'an."

Riyad as-Salihin, hadith number 993

HADITHS ON TRUE FAITH

سَأَلَ رَجُلٌ رَسُولَ اللهِ صَلَّى اللهُ عَلَيْهِ وَسَلَّمَ أَىُّ الإِسْلامَ خَيْرٌ قَالَ " تُطْعِمُ الطَّعَامَ وَتَقْرَأُ السَّلاَمَ عَلَى مَنْ عَرَفْتَ وَمَنْ لَمْ تَعْرِفْ " .

A man asked the Messenger of Allah (ﷺ), "Which aspect of Islam is the most important?" He replied, "That you should feed and greet both those you know and those you do not know."

Sunan Abu Dawûd, hadith number 5194

قَالَ رَسُولُ اللهِ صَلَّى اللهُ عَلَيْهِ وَسَلَّمَ " لاَ تَبَاغَضُوا وَلاَ تَحَاسَدُوا وَلاَ تَدَابَرُوا وَكُونُوا عِبَادَ اللهِ إِخْوَانًا وَلاَ يَحِلُّ لِمُسْلِمٍ أَنْ يَهْجُرَ أَخَاهُ فَوْقَ ثَلاثٍ".

The Messenger of Allah (ﷺ) said, "Do not hate one another, do not envy one another, do not turn away from one another, but rather be servants of Allah as brothers. It is not lawful for a Muslim to boycott his brother for more than three days."

Sahih Muslim, hadith number 2558 b

قَالَ رَسُولُ اللهِ صَلَّى اللهُ عَلَيْهِ وَسَلَّمَ " مَثَلُ المُؤْمِنِينَ في تَوَادِّهِمْ وتَرَاحُمِهِمْ وتَعَاطُفِهِمْ، مَثَلُ الجَسَدِ إذا اشْتَكَى مِنْهُ عُضْوٌ تَدَاعَى له سَائِرُ الجَسَدِ بِالسَّهَرِ والحُمَّى ".

The Messenger of Allah (ﷺ) said, "The believers are like one body in their mutual kindness, compassion and sympathy. If one part suffers, the whole body reacts with sleeplessness and fever."

Riyad as-Salihin, hadith number 224

HADITHS ON TRUE FAITH

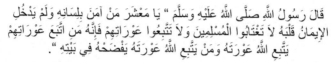

قَالَ رَسُولُ اللهِ صَلَّى اللهُ عَلَيْهِ وَسَلَّمَ " يَا مَعْشَرَ مَنْ آمَنَ بِلِسَانِهِ وَلَمْ يَدْخُلِ
الإِيمَانُ قَلْبَهُ لاَ تَغْتَابُوا الْمُسْلِمِينَ وَلاَ تَتَّبِعُوا عَوْرَاتِهِمْ فَإِنَّهُ مَنِ اتَّبَعَ عَوْرَاتِهِمْ
يَتَّبِعِ اللهُ عَوْرَتَهُ وَمَنْ يَتَّبِعِ اللهُ عَوْرَتَهُ يَفْضَحْهُ فِي بَيْتِهِ ".

The Prophet (ﷺ) said, "O assembly of those who have believed
with their tongues while faith has not yet entered their hearts!
Do not backbite Muslims, and do not search for their faults.
For whoever searches for their faults, Allah will search for
his faults, and if Allah searches for someone's faults, He will
expose him even if he is in the privacy of his own home."

Sunan Abu Dawûd, hadith number 4880

سَمِعتَ رَسُولَ اللهِ صَلَّى اللهُ عَلَيْهِ وَسَلَّمَ يَقُولُ " أَرَأَيْتُمْ لَوْ أَنَّ نَهَرًا بِبَابِ أَحَدِكُمْ،
يَغْتَسِلُ فِيهِ كُلَّ يَوْمٍ خَمْسًا، مَا تَقُولُ ذَلِكَ يُبْقِي مِنْ دَرَنِهِ ". قَالُوا لاَ يُبْقِي مِنْ
دَرَنِهِ شَيْئًا. قَالَ " فَذَلِكَ مِثْلُ الصَّلَوَاتِ الْخَمْسِ، يَمْحُو اللهُ بِهَا الْخَطَايَا ".

I heard the Messenger of Allah (ﷺ) saying, "If one of you had a
river in front of his door and bathed in it five times a day, would
you notice any trace of filth in him?" They said, "There would be
no trace of dirt left" The Prophet (ﷺ) added, "This is the example
of the five prayers with which Allah eradicates evil deeds."

Sahih Al-Bukhari, hadith number 528

HADITHS ON TRUE FAITH

قَالَ رَسُولُ اللهِ صَلَّى اللهُ عَلَيْهِ وَسَلَّمَ " تُعْرَضُ الْأَعْمَالُ فِي كُلِّ يَوْمِ خَمِيسٍ وَاثْنَيْنِ فَيَغْفِرُ
اللهُ عَزَّ وَجَلَّ فِي ذَلِكَ الْيَوْمِ لِكُلِّ امْرِئٍ لاَ يُشْرِكُ بِاللهِ شَيْئًا إِلاَّ امْرَأً كَانَتْ بَيْنَهُ وَبَيْنَ
أَخِيهِ شَحْنَاءُ فَيُقَالُ ارْكُوا هَذَيْنِ حَتَّى يَصْطَلِحَا ارْكُوا هَذَيْنِ حَتَّى يَصْطَلِحَا ".

The Messenger of Allah (ﷺ) said "The deeds (of His servants)
are recited to Allah, Exalted and Glorious, every Thursday
and every Monday, and He forgives every person who
does not associate with Him, except the one in whose
heart there is resentment against his brother. It will be
said: Set aside his case until they are reconciled".

Sahih Muslim, hadith number 2565 c

[...] أَنَّ النَّبِيَّ ـ صَلَّى اللهُ عَلَيْهِ وَسَلَّمَ ـ دَخَلَ عَلَى شَابٍّ وَهُوَ فِي الْمَوْتِ فَقَالَ : " كَيْفَ تَجِدُكَ
" . قَالَ : أَرْجُو اللهَ يَا رَسُولَ اللهِ وَأَخَافُ ذُنُوبِي . فَقَالَ رَسُولُ اللهِ ـ صَلَّى اللهُ عَلَيْهِ وَسَلَّمَ ـ :
" لاَ يَجْتَمِعَانِ فِي قَلْبِ عَبْدٍ فِي مِثْلِ هَذَا الْمَوْطِنِ إِلاَّ أَعْطَاهُ اللهُ مَا يَرْجُو وَآمَنَهُ مِمَّا يَخَافُ ".

[...] The Prophet came to a young man who was dying and
asked him, "How are you?" He said, "I have hope in Allah, O
Messenger of Allah, but I fear my sins." The Messenger of Allah
(ﷺ) said, "These two things (hope and fear) cannot coexist in
the heart of a person in such a situation, but Allah will give
him what he hopes for and protect him from what he fears."

Sunan Ibn Mayah, hadith number 4261

HADITHS ON TRUE FAITH

قَالَ رَسُولُ اللَّهِ صَلَّى اللَّهُ عَلَيْهِ وَسَلَّمَ " أَصْدَقُ بَيْتٍ قَالَهُ الشَّاعِرُ أَلاَ كُلُّ شَيْءٍ مَا خَلاَ اللَّهَ بَاطِلُ ".

The Prophet (ﷺ) said, "The truest poetic verse ever uttered by a poet is: Indeed, everything other than Allah is falsehood".

Sahih Al-Bukhari, hadith number 6489

قَالَ رَسُولُ اللَّهِ صَلَّى اللَّهُ عَلَيْهِ وَسَلَّمَ " لَمَّا قَضَى اللَّهُ الْخَلْقَ كَتَبَ فِي كِتَابِهِ، فَهُوَ عِنْدَهُ فَوْقَ الْعَرْشِ إِنَّ رَحْمَتِي غَلَبَتْ غَضَبِي".

The Messenger of Allah (ﷺ) said, "When Allah completed the creation, He wrote in His Book, which is next to Him on His Throne, 'My mercy precedes My wrath.'"

Sahih Al-Bukhari, hadith number 3194

قَالَ رَسُولُ اللَّهِ صَلَّى اللَّهُ عَلَيْهِ وَسَلَّمَ " إِنَّ اللَّهَ يَقُولُ أَنَا عِنْدَ ظَنِّ عَبْدِي فِيَّ وَأَنَا مَعَهُ إِذَا دَعَانِي".

The Messenger of Allah (ﷺ) said, "Allah the Exalted says, 'I am as My servant thinks of Me, and I am with him when he calls upon Me.'"

Yam'a Al Tirmidhi, hadith number 2388

HADITHS ON TRUE FAITH

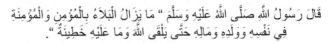

قَالَ رَسُولُ اللهِ صَلَّى اللهُ عَلَيْهِ وَسَلَّمَ " مَا يَزَالُ الْبَلَاءُ بِالْمُؤْمِنِ وَالْمُؤْمِنَةِ
فِي نَفْسِهِ وَوَلَدِهِ وَمَالِهِ حَتَّى يَلْقَى اللهَ وَمَا عَلَيْهِ خَطِيئَةٌ ".

The Messenger of Allah (ﷺ) said, "The affliction will continue to affect the believer in the believer's child, self, and wealth until they meet Allah, and there will be no sin for them."

Yam'a Al Tirmidhi, hadith number 2399

قَالَ رَسُولُ اللَّهِ صَلَّى اللهُ عَلَيْهِ وَسَلَّمَ " إِنَّ الدِّينَ يُسْرٌ، وَلَنْ يُشَادَّ الدِّينَ أَحَدٌ إِلاَّ غَلَبَهُ،
فَسَدِّدُوا وَقَارِبُوا وَأَبْشِرُوا، وَاسْتَعِينُوا بِالْغَدْوَةِ وَالرَّوْحَةِ وَشَيْءٍ مِنَ الدُّلْجَةِ ".

The Prophet (ﷺ) said, "Indeed, the religion is easy, and no one overburdens himself in his religion except that it will overpower him. So you shouldn't be extremists, but try to be near to perfection and receive the good tidings that you will be rewarded; and gain strength by worshipping in the mornings, the afternoons, and during the nights."

Sahih Al-Bukhari, hadith number 39

[...] سَمِعْتُ رَسُولَ اللَّهِ ـ صَلَّى اللهُ عَلَيْهِ وَسَلَّمَ ـ يَقُولُ " مَا مَثَلُ الدُّنْيَا فِي
الْآخِرَةِ إِلاَّ مَثَلُ مَا يَجْعَلُ أَحَدُكُمْ إِصْبَعَهُ فِي الْيَمِّ فَلْيَنْظُرْ بِمَ يَرْجِعُ".

"[...] I heard the Messenger of Allah (ﷺ) say, "Compared to the Hereafter, this world is like when one of you dips his finger in the sea, how much water do you think will be left on his finger? "

Sunan Ibn Mayah, hadith number 4108

HADITHS ON TRUE FAITH

قَالَ رَسُولُ اللهِ صَلَّى اللهُ عَلَيْهِ وَسَلَّمَ " مَنْ يُحْرَمِ الرِّفْقَ يُحْرَمِ الْخَيْرَ ".

The Messenger of Allah (ﷺ) said, "Whoever is deprived of gentleness is deprived of goodness."

Sunan Ibn Mayah, hadith number 3687

سُئِلَ النَّبِيُّ صَلَّى اللهُ عَلَيْهِ وَسَلَّمَ أَيُّ الأَعْمَالِ أَفْضَلُ قَالَ " طُولُ الْقِيَامِ ". قِيلَ فَأَيُّ الصَّدَقَةِ أَفْضَلُ قَالَ " جُهْدُ الْمُقِلِّ".

They asked the Prophet (ﷺ): "Which of the deeds is better? He replied: Standing for a long time (in prayer). They asked him again: Which charity is better? He replied: Charity given by a man who possesses a small fortune which he has earned by his work."

Sunan Abu Dawûd, hadith number 1449

قَالَ رَسُولُ اللهِ صَلَّى اللهُ عَلَيْهِ وَسَلَّمَ " مَنْ قَالَ فِي كِتَابِ اللهِ عَزَّ وَجَلَّ بِرَأْيِهِ فَأَصَابَ فَقَدْ أَخْطَأَ " .

The Prophet (ﷺ) said, "If anyone interprets the Book of Allah in the light of his own opinion, even if he is right, he is still wrong."

Sunan Abu Dawûd, hadith number 3652

HADITHS ON TRUE FAITH

قَالَ رَسُولُ اللَّهِ صَلَّى اللَّهُ عَلَيْهِ وَسَلَّمَ " مَنْ نَفَّسَ عَنْ مُؤْمِنٍ كُرْبَةً مِنْ كُرَبِ الدُّنْيَا نَفَّسَ اللَّهُ عَنْهُ كُرْبَةً مِنْ كُرَبِ يَوْمِ الْقِيَامَةِ وَمَنْ يَسَّرَ عَلَى مُعْسِرٍ يَسَّرَ اللَّهُ عَلَيْهِ فِي الدُّنْيَا وَالْآخِرَةِ وَمَنْ سَتَرَ مُسْلِمًا سَتَرَهُ اللَّهُ فِي الدُّنْيَا وَالْآخِرَةِ وَاللَّهُ فِي عَوْنِ الْعَبْدِ مَا كَانَ الْعَبْدُ فِي عَوْنِ أَخِيهِ وَمَنْ سَلَكَ طَرِيقًا يَلْتَمِسُ فِيهِ عِلْمًا سَهَّلَ اللَّهُ لَهُ بِهِ طَرِيقًا إِلَى الْجَنَّةِ وَمَا اجْتَمَعَ قَوْمٌ فِي بَيْتٍ مِنْ بُيُوتِ اللَّهِ يَتْلُونَ كِتَابَ اللَّهِ وَيَتَدَارَسُونَهُ بَيْنَهُمْ إِلاَّ نَزَلَتْ عَلَيْهِمُ السَّكِينَةُ وَغَشِيَتْهُمُ الرَّحْمَةُ وَحَفَّتْهُمُ الْمَلاَئِكَةُ وَذَكَرَهُمُ اللَّهُ فِيمَنْ عِنْدَهُ وَمَنْ بَطَّأَ بِهِ عَمَلُهُ لَمْ يُسْرِعْ بِهِ نَسَبُهُ ".

The Prophet (ﷺ) said, "Whoever relieves a believer from one of the hardships of this world, Allah will relieve him from one of the hardships of the Day of Judgment. Whoever makes things easy for someone in difficulty, Allah will make things easy for him in this world and the Hereafter. Whoever conceals the faults of a Muslim, Allah will conceal his faults in this world and the Hereafter. Allah helps His servant as long as the servant helps his brother. Whoever treads a path seeking knowledge, Allah will make easy for him the path to Paradise. People do not gather in the houses of Allah, reciting the Book of Allah and studying it together, except that tranquility descends upon them, mercy covers them, angels surround them, and Allah mentions them among those who are with Him. And whoever is reluctant in doing good deeds, his lineage will not make him go ahead."

Sahih Muslim, hadith number 2699

HADITHS ON TRUE FAITH

قَالَ رَسُولُ اللهِ صَلَّى اللهُ عَلَيْهِ وَسَلَّمَ " يَعْقِدُ الشَّيْطَانُ عَلَى قَافِيَةِ رَأْسِ أَحَدِكُمْ إِذَا هُوَ نَامَ ثَلاثَ عُقَدٍ، يَضْرِبُ كُلَّ عُقْدَةٍ مَكَانَهَا عَلَيْكَ لَيْلٌ طَوِيلٌ فَارْقُدْ. فَإِنِ اسْتَيْقَظَ فَذَكَرَ اللهَ انْحَلَّتْ عُقْدَةٌ، فَإِنْ تَوَضَّأَ انْحَلَّتْ عُقْدَةٌ، فَإِنْ صَلَّى انْحَلَّتْ عُقَدُهُ كُلُّهَا، فَأَصْبَحَ نَشِيطًا طَيِّبَ النَّفْسِ، وَإِلاَّ أَصْبَحَ خَبِيثَ النَّفْسِ كَسْلاَنَ ".

The Messenger of Allah (ﷺ) said, "While you are sleeping, Satan ties three knots on the back of the neck of each of you, and to each knot he says the following words, ‹The night is long, so go back to sleep.› When that person wakes up and celebrates the praises of Allah, one knot is untied, and when he makes ablution, the second knot is untied, and when he prays, all the knots are untied, and he gets up in the morning cheerful and in a good mood. Otherwise, he rises dejected and sluggish."

Sahih Al-Bukhari, hadith number 3269

عَنْ مُعَاوِيَةَ، أَنَّ النَّبِيَّ صَلَّى اللهُ عَلَيْهِ وَسَلَّمَ نَهَى عَنِ الْغُلُوطَاتِ.

Mu'awia reported that the Prophet (ﷺ) forbade the discussion of sensitive topics.

Sunan Abu Dawûd, hadith number 3656

HADITHS ON TRUE FAITH

عَنْ أَنَسٍ، أَنَّ نَفَرًا، مِنْ أَصْحَابِ النَّبِيِّ صَلَّى اللهُ عَلَيْهِ وَسَلَّمَ قَالَ بَعْضُهُمْ لاَ أَتَزَوَّجُ النِّسَاءَ . وَقَالَ بَعْضُهُمْ لاَ آكُلُ اللَّحْمَ . وَقَالَ بَعْضُهُمْ لاَ أَنَامُ عَلَى فِرَاشٍ . وَقَالَ بَعْضُهُمْ أَصُومُ فَلاَ أُفْطِرُ . فَبَلَغَ ذَلِكَ رَسُولَ اللهِ صلى الله عليه وسلم فَحَمِدَ اللهَ وَأَثْنَى عَلَيْهِ ثُمَّ قَالَ " مَا بَالُ أَقْوَامٍ يَقُولُونَ كَذَا وَكَذَا لَكِنِّي أُصَلِّي وَأَنَامُ وَأَصُومُ وَأُفْطِرُ وَأَتَزَوَّجُ النِّسَاءَ فَمَنْ رَغِبَ عَنْ سُنَّتِي فَلَيْسَ مِنِّي ".

Anas reported that some companions of the Prophet (ﷺ) said, "I will not marry women," and some said, "I will not eat meat," and some said, "I will not lie down in bed," and some said, "I will fast and not break my fast." The news reached the Prophet (ﷺ), and he praised Allah, thanked Him, and then said, "What has happened to the people that they say such and such? But I observe prayer and sleep too. I observe fast and break it, and I marry women. Whoever turns away from my Sunnah is not from me."

Sunan Al-Nasa'i, hadith number 3217

قَالَ رَسُولُ اللهِ صَلَّى اللهُ عَلَيْهِ وَسَلَّمَ "مَنِ اتَّبَعَ جَنَازَةَ مُسْلِمٍ إِيمَانًا وَاحْتِسَابًا فَصَلَّى عَلَيْهِ ثُمَّ انْتَظَرَ حَتَّى يُوضَعَ فِي قَبْرِهِ كَانَ لَهُ قِيرَاطَانِ أَحَدُهُمَا مِثْلُ أُحُدٍ وَمَنْ صَلَّى عَلَيْهِ ثُمَّ رَجَعَ كَانَ لَهُ قِيرَاطٌ".

The Prophet (ﷺ) said, "Whoever follows a Muslim's funeral procession, believing in Allah and seeking His reward, and offers the funeral prayer for him, will get a reward equal to two Qirats. Each Qirat is like the size of Mount Uhud. Whoever offers the funeral prayer and then returns before the deceased is buried, he will have one Qirat."

Sunan Al-Nasa'i, hadith number 5032

HADITHS ON TRUE FAITH

سَمِعْتُ رَسُولَ اللَّهِ صَلَّى اللَّهُ عَلَيْهِ وَسَلَّمَ يَقُولُ " مَنْ رَآنِي فِي الْمَنَامِ فَسَيَرَانِي فِي الْيَقْظَةِ " وَلاَ يَتَمَثَّلُ الشَّيْطَانُ بِي ".

I heard Allah's Messenger (ﷺ) say, "Whoever sees me in dreams really sees me, for the devil does not take my form."

Sunan Abu Dawûd, hadith number 5023

قَالَ رَسُولُ اللَّهِ صَلَّى اللَّهُ عَلَيْهِ وَسَلَّمَ " الطُّهُورُ شَطْرُ الإِيمَانِ وَالْحَمْدُ لِلَّهِ تَمْلأُ الْمِيزَانَ. وَسُبْحَانَ اللَّهِ وَالْحَمْدُ لِلَّهِ تَمْلآَنِ مَا بَيْنَ السَّمَوَاتِ وَالأَرْضِ وَالصَّلاَةُ نُورٌ وَالصَّدَقَةُ بُرْهَانٌ وَالصَّبْرُ ضِيَاءٌ وَالْقُرْآنُ حُجَّةٌ لَكَ أَوْ عَلَيْكَ كُلُّ النَّاسِ يَغْدُو فَبَائِعٌ نَفْسَهُ فَمُعْتِقُهَا أَوْ مُوبِقُهَا " .

The Prophet (ﷺ) said, "Purification is half of faith, and Alhamdulillah (praise be to Allah) fills the scale. SubhanAllah (glory be to Allah) and Alhamdulillah fill up what is between the heavens and the earth. Prayer is a light, charity is proof, and patience is illumination. The Qur'an is a plea in your favor or against you. All people go out early in the morning and sell themselves, freeing or destroying themselves."

Sahih Muslim, hadith number 223

" [...] قُلتُ: يا نَبِيَّ اللهِ عَلِّمْنِي شيئًا أَنْتَفِعُ به، قالَ: " اعْزِلِ الأَذَى عن طَرِيقِ المُسْلِمِينَ ".

" [...] I said, 'O Prophet of Allah, teach me something that I can benefit from.' He said, "Remove the harmful things from the path of the Muslims. ""

Sunan Ibn Mayah, hadith number 3681

HADITHS ON TRUE FAITH

قَالَ رَسُولُ اللهِ صَلَّى اللهُ عَلَيْهِ وَسَلَّمَ " سَبْعَةٌ يُظِلُّهُمُ اللهُ فِي ظِلِّهِ يَوْمَ لاَ ظِلَّ إِلاَّ ظِلُّهُ إِمَامٌ عَادِلٌ وَشَابٌ نَشَأَ بِعِبَادَةِ اللهِ وَرَجُلٌ كَانَ قَلْبُهُ مُعَلَّقًا بِالْمَسْجِدِ إِذَا خَرَجَ مِنْهُ حَتَّى يَعُودَ إِلَيْهِ وَرَجُلاَنِ تَحَابَّا فِي اللهِ فَاجْتَمَعَا عَلَى ذَلِكَ وَتَفَرَّقَا وَرَجُلٌ ذَكَرَ اللهَ خَالِيًا فَفَاضَتْ عَيْنَاهُ وَرَجُلٌ دَعَتْهُ امْرَأَةٌ ذَاتُ حَسَبٍ وَجَمَالٍ فَقَالَ إِنِّي أَخَافُ اللهَ وَرَجُلٌ تَصَدَّقَ بِصَدَقَةٍ فَأَخْفَاهَا حَتَّى لاَ تَعْلَمَ شِمَالُهُ مَا تُنْفِقُ يَمِينُهُ ".

The Messenger of Allah (ﷺ) said, "Seven will find refuge in the shadow of Allah on the day when there will be no shadow but His shadow: An upright Imam, a young man who has been brought up to worship Allah, a man whose heart is attached to the mosque when he leaves it until he returns to it, two men who love each other for Allah, who come together and part for Him, a man who remembers Allah in silence and whose eyes swell with tears, a man who is invited by a woman of rank and beauty, but says: 'I fear Allah, Mighty and Exalted,' and a man who conceals the alms he gives so that his left hand does not know what his right hand has spent."

Sahih Al Tirmidhi, hadith number 2391

قَالَ رَسُولُ اللهِ صَلَّى اللهُ عَلَيْهِ وَسَلَّمَ "هلك المتنطعون" قالها ثلاثاً .

The Prophet (ﷺ) said, "Ruined are those who insist on strictness in matters of faith." He repeated it three times.

Riyad As-Salihin, hadith number 144

HADITHS ON TRUE FAITH

قَالَ رَسُولُ اللَّهِ صَلَّى اللَّهُ عَلَيْهِ وَسَلَّمَ " مَا مِنْ شَيْءٍ أَثْقَلُ فِي الْمِيزَانِ مِنْ حُسْنِ الْخُلُقِ ".

The Prophet (ﷺ) said, "There is nothing heavier than
a good character that will be placed in the scales
of a believer on the Day of Resurrection."

Sunan Abu Dawûd, hadith number 4799

قَالَ رَسُولُ اللَّهِ صَلَّى اللَّهُ عَلَيْهِ وَسَلَّمَ " مَنْ أَطَاعَنِي فَقَدْ أَطَاعَ اللَّهَ وَمَنْ عَصَانِي فَقَدْ عَصَى اللَّهَ ".

The Prophet (ﷺ) said, "Whoever obeys me, obeys
Allah, and whoever disobeys me, disobeys Allah."

Sunan Ibn Mayah, hadith number 3

قَالَ النَّبِيُّ صَلَّى اللَّهُ عَلَيْهِ وَسَلَّمَ " الْبِرُّ حُسْنُ الْخُلُقِ وَالإِثْمُ مَا
حَاكَ فِي نَفْسِكَ وَكَرِهْتَ أَنْ يَطَّلِعَ عَلَيْهِ النَّاسُ ".

The Prophet (ﷺ) said, "Righteousness is a good
character, and sin is what wavers in your soul and
you dislike for people to find out about it."

Sahih Al Tirmidhi, hadith number 2389

HADITHS ON PROPER BEHAVIOR

قَالَ رَسُولُ اللَّهِ صَلَّى اللَّهُ عَلَيْهِ وَسَلَّمَ " إِنَّ أَوْلَى النَّاسِ بِاللَّهِ مَنْ بَدَأَهُمْ بِالسَّلَامِ ".

The Messenger of Allah (ﷺ) said "The closest to Allah among the people are those who initiate greetings of peace."

Sunan Abu Dawûd, hadith number 5197

كان النبيُّ صَلَّى اللَّهُ عَلَيْهِ وَسَلَّمَ إذا ذهبَ إلى الغائطِ أَبْعَدَ.

When the Prophet (ﷺ) went out to relieve himself, he went to a distant place.

Sunan Abu Dawûd, hadith number 1

سَأَلَ رجلُ النَّبِيَّ صَلَّى اللَّهُ عَلَيْهِ وَسَلَّمَ أَيُّ الإِسْلَامِ خَيْرٌ قَالَ صَلَّى اللَّهُ عَلَيْهِ وَسَلَّمَ " تُطْعِمُ الطَّعَامَ، وَتَقْرَأُ السَّلَامَ عَلَى مَنْ عَرَفْتَ، وَعَلَى مَنْ لَمْ تَعْرِفْ ".

A man asked the Prophet (ﷺ), "What Islamic qualities are the best?", the Prophet (ﷺ) said, "Feed the people and greet those you know and those you do not know."

Sahih Al-Bukhari, hadith number 6236

قَالَ رَسُولُ اللَّهِ صَلَّى اللَّهُ عَلَيْهِ وَسَلَّمَ " لَا تَأْكُلُوا بِالشِّمَالِ فَإِنَّ الشَّيْطَانَ يَأْكُلُ بِالشِّمَالِ ".

The Messenger of Allah (ﷺ) said, "Do not eat with the left hand, for Satan eats with the left."

Sahih Muslim, hadith number 2019

HADITHS ON PROPER BEHAVIOR

قَالَ رَسُولُ اللَّهِ صَلَّى اللَّهُ عَلَيْهِ وَسَلَّمَ " يُسَلِّمُ الرَّاكِبُ عَلَى الْمَاشِي وَالْمَاشِي عَلَى الْقَاعِدِ، وَالْقَلِيلُ عَلَى الْكَثِيرِ ".

The Messenger of Allah (ﷺ) said, "The rider should greet the one who walks, and the one who walks should greet the one who sits, and the small number of people should greet the large number of people."

Sahih Al-Bukhari, hadith number 6233

قَالَ النَّبِيُّ صَلَّى اللَّهُ عَلَيْهِ وَسَلَّمَ " لاَ تُبَاشِرِ الْمَرْأَةُ الْمَرْأَةَ فَتَنْعَتَهَا لِزَوْجِهَا، كَأَنَّهُ يَنْظُرُ إِلَيْهَا ".

The Prophet (ﷺ) said, "A woman should not look at another woman and describe her to her husband as if he is looking at her."

Sahih Al-Bukhari, hadith number 5240

قَالَ رَسُولُ اللَّهِ صَلَّى اللَّهُ عَلَيْهِ وَسَلَّمَ " لاَ يَبُولَنَّ أَحَدُكُمْ فِي الْمَاءِ الدَّائِمِ وَلاَ يَغْتَسِلْ فِيهِ مِنَ الْجَنَابَةِ ".

The Messenger of Allah (ﷺ) said, "None of you should urinate in stagnant water and wash in it after sexual impurity."

Sunan Abu Dawûd, hadith number 70

HADITHS ON PROPER BEHAVIOR

عَنْ جَرِيرٍ، قَالَ سَأَلْتُ رَسُولَ اللَّهِ صَلَّى اللَّهُ عَلَيْهِ وَسَلَّمَ عَنْ نَظْرَةِ الْفَجْأَةِ (إلى المرأة) فَقَالَ " اصْرِفْ بَصَرَكَ ".

Jarir said: I asked the Messenger of Allah (ﷺ) about an accidental, unintentional glance (at a woman). He (ﷺ) said, "Look away."

Sunan Abu Dawûd, hadith number 2148

قَالَ رَسُولُ اللَّهِ صَلَّى اللَّهُ عَلَيْهِ وَسَلَّمَ لِعَلِيٍّ " يَا عَلِيُّ لاَ تُتْبِعِ النَّظْرَةَ النَّظْرَةَ (إلى المرأة) فَإِنَّ لَكَ الأُولَى (لأنها وقعت بدون قصد) وَلَيْسَتْ لَكَ الآخِرَةُ ".

The Prophet (ﷺ) said to Ali: "Do not take a second look (at a woman), for while you are not to blame for the first (because it was unintentional), you are not entitled to the second."

Sunan Abu Dawûd, hadith number 2149

قَالَ رَسُولُ اللَّهِ صَلَّى اللَّهُ عَلَيْهِ وَسَلَّمَ " يُسَلِّمُ الصَّغِيرُ عَلَى الْكَبِيرِ وَالْمَارُّ عَلَى الْقَاعِدِ وَالْقَلِيلُ عَلَى الْكَثِيرِ " .

The Messenger of Allah (ﷺ) said "The young should greet the old, the person passing by should greet the person sitting, and a small group should greet the larger group first."

Sunan Abu Dawûd, hadith number 5198

HADITHS ON PROPER BEHAVIOR

قَالَتْ عَائِشَةُ ـ رضى الله عنها ـ كَانَ أَصْحَابُ رَسُولِ اللَّهِ صَلَّى اللَّهُ عَلَيْهِ وَسَلَّمَ عُمَّالَ أَنْفُسِهِمْ، وَكَانَ يَكُونُ لَهُمْ أَرْوَاحٌ فَقِيلَ لَهُمْ لَوِ اغْتَسَلْتُمْ.

Aisha narrated, "The companions of the Messenger of Allah (ﷺ) performed physical labor so their sweat smelled and they were advised to bathe."

Sahih Al-Bukhari, hadith number 2071

قَالَ النَّبِيُّ صَلَّى اللَّهُ عَلَيْهِ وَسَلَّمَ " سَدِّدُوا وَقَارِبُوا، وَأَبْشِرُوا، فَإِنَّهُ لاَ يُدْخِلُ أَحَدًا الْجَنَّةَ عَمَلُهُ." قَالُوا وَلاَ، أَنْتَ يَا رَسُولَ اللَّهِ قَالَ " وَلاَ أَنَا إِلاَّ أَنْ يَتَغَمَّدَنِي اللَّهُ بِمَغْفِرَةٍ وَرَحْمَةٍ ".

The Prophet (ﷺ) said, "Do good deeds rightly, with sincerity and moderation. Receive good news, for none will enter Paradise due to his deeds alone." They asked, "Not even you, O Messenger of Allah?" He replied, "Not even me, unless Allah envelops me in His forgiveness and mercy."

Sahih Al-Bukhari, hadith number 6467

HADITHS ON PROPER BEHAVIOR

قَالَ رَسُولُ اللَّهِ صَلَّى اللَّهُ عَلَيْهِ وَسَلَّمَ " [...] بَلِ ائْتَمِرُوا بِالْمَعْرُوفِ وَتَنَاهَوْا عَنِ الْمُنْكَرِ حَتَّى إِذَا رَأَيْتَ شُحًّا مُطَاعًا وَهَوًى مُتَّبَعًا وَدُنْيَا مُؤْثَرَةً وَإِعْجَابَ كُلِّ ذِي رَأْيٍ بِرَأْيِهِ وَرَأَيْتَ أَمْرًا لاَ يَدَانِ لَكَ بِهِ فَعَلَيْكَ خُوَيْصَّةَ نَفْسِكَ وَدَعْ أَمْرَ الْعَوَامِّ فَإِنَّ مِنْ وَرَائِكُمْ أَيَّامَ الصَّبْرِ الصَّبْرُ فِيهِنَّ مِثْلُ قَبْضٍ عَلَى الْجَمْرِ لِلْعَامِلِ فِيهِنَّ مِثْلُ أَجْرِ خَمْسِينَ رَجُلاً يَعْمَلُونَ بِمِثْلِ عَمَلِهِ " .

The Messenger of Allah (ﷺ) said: [...] "Command one another what is good and forbid one another what is evil. But when you see that greed is rife, and covetousness follows, and this world is preferred to the Hereafter, and everyone is proud of his own opinion, and you realize that you are powerless against it, then you should mind your own business and leave the common people to their own devices. After you, will come days of patience, when patience will be like grasping a burning ember, and whoever does a good deed will be rewarded like fifty men doing the same deed."

Sunan Ibn Mayah, hadith number 4014

عَنْ أَنَسِ بْنِ مَالِكٍ ـ رضى الله عنه أَنَّهُ مَرَّ عَلَى صِبْيَانٍ فَسَلَّمَ عَلَيْهِمْ وَقَالَ "كَانَ النَّبِيُّ صلى الله عليه وسلم يَفْعَلُهُ".

Anas bin Malik related that he passed by a group of boys, greeted them and said, "The Prophet (ﷺ) used to do this."

Sahih Al-Bukhari, hadith number 6247

HADITHS ON PROPER BEHAVIOR

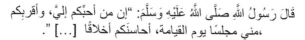

قَالَ رَسُولُ اللهِ صَلَّى اللهُ عَلَيْهِ وَسَلَّمَ: "إن من أحبّكم إلَيَّ، وأقربِكم مني مجلسًا يوم القيامة، أحاسنكم أخلاقًا [...] " .

The Messenger of Allah (ﷺ) said, "Those who are dearest to me and those who will be closest to me on the Day of Resurrection are those who are on their best behavior [...]."

Riyad As-Salihin, hadith number 1738

عَنْ أَنَس قَالَ: "كَانَ النَّبِيُّ صَلَّى اللهُ عَلَيْهِ وَسَلَّمَ إِذَا تَكَلَّمَ بِكَلِمَةٍ أَعَادَهَا ثَلَاثًا حَتَّى تُفْهَمَ عَنْهُ وَإِذَا أَتَى عَلَى قَوْمٍ فَسَلَّمَ عَلَيْهِمْ سَلَّمَ عَلَيْهِمْ ثَلَاثًا " .

Anas said, "When the Prophet (ﷺ) made a statement, he would repeat it three times so that it would be understood, and that when he met a company and greeted them, he would do so three times."

Mishkát al-Masabíh, hadith number 208

قَالَ رَسُولُ اللهِ صَلَّى اللهُ عَلَيْهِ وَسَلَّمَ " إِنَّ فُسْطَاطَ الْمُسْلِمِينَ يَوْمَ الْمَلْحَمَةِ بِالْغُوطَةِ إِلَى جَانِبِ مَدِينَةٍ يُقَالُ لَهَا دِمَشْقُ مِنْ خَيْرِ مَدَائِنِ الشَّامِ " .

The Prophet (ﷺ) said, "The gathering place of the Muslims at the time of war will be at al-Gutah, near a city called Damascus, one of the best cities in Syria."

Sunan Abu Dawûd, hadith number 4298

HADITHS ON PROPER BEHAVIOR

مَا ضَرَبَ رَسُولُ اللَّهِ صَلَّى اللَّهُ عَلَيْهِ وَسَلَّمَ خَادِمًا وَلاَ امْرَأَةً قَطُّ.

The Messenger of Allah (ﷺ) never beat a servant or a woman.

Sunan Abu Dawûd, hadith number 4786

قَالَ النَّبِيُّ صَلَّى اللَّهُ عَلَيْهِ وَسَلَّمَ " مَنْ كَانَ يُؤْمِنُ بِاللَّهِ وَالْيَوْمِ الآخِرِ فَلْيُحْسِنْ إِلَى جَارِهِ وَمَنْ كَانَ
يُؤْمِنُ بِاللَّهِ وَالْيَوْمِ الآخِرِ فَلْيُكْرِمْ ضَيْفَهُ وَمَنْ كَانَ يُؤْمِنُ بِاللَّهِ وَالْيَوْمِ الآخِرِ فَلْيَقُلْ خَيْرًا أَوْ لِيَسْكُتْ " .

The Prophet (ﷺ) said, "Whoever believes in Allah and
the Judgment Day should treat his neighbor well.
Whoever believes in Allah and the Last Day should
honor his guest. Whoever believes in Allah and the Last
Day should say something good or keep silent."

Sunan Ibn Mayah, hadith number 3672

اسْتَأْذَنَ رجلٌ عَلَى النَّبِيِّ صلى الله عليه وسلم فَقَالَ النَّبِيُّ صلى الله عليه وسلم " بِئْسَ أَخُو الْعَشِيرَةِ " .
فَلَمَّا دَخَلَ انْبَسَطَ إِلَيْهِ رَسُولُ اللَّهِ صلى الله عليه وسلم وَكَلَّمَهُ فَلَمَّا خَرَجَ قُلْتُ يَا رَسُولَ اللَّهِ لَمَّا اسْتَأْذَنَ قُلْتَ
" بِئْسَ أَخُو الْعَشِيرَةِ " . فَلَمَّا دَخَلَ انْبَسَطْتَ إِلَيْهِ . فَقَالَ " يَا عَائِشَةُ إِنَّ اللَّهَ لاَ يُحِبُّ الْفَاحِشَ الْمُتَفَحِّشَ " .

A man asked permission to see the Prophet (ﷺ); and the
Prophet (ﷺ) remarked, "What a bad tribesman he is!" When
he entered, the Messenger of Allah (ﷺ) treated him with
sincerity and kindness and spoke to him. When he left, Aisha
said to him, 'Messenger of Allah! When he asked permission,
you said, 'He is a bad tribesman, but when he entered, you
treated him openly and kindly.' The Messenger of Allah
(ﷺ) replied, "O Aisha, indeed, Allah does not love those
who indulge in foul language and indecent conduct."

Sunan Abu Dawûd, hadith number 4792

HADITHS ON PROPER BEHAVIOR

قَالَ رَسُولُ اللهِ صلى الله عليه وسلم " اتَّقِ اللهَ حَيْثُمَا كُنْتَ وَأَتْبِعِ
السَّيِّئَةَ الْحَسَنَةَ تَمْحُهَا وَخَالِقِ النَّاسَ بِخُلُقٍ حَسَنٍ ".

Messenger of Allah (ﷺ) said, "Fear Allah wherever
you are, follow a bad deed with a good deed so
that it will nullify it, and treat people well."

Sahih Al Tirmidhi, hadith number 1987

.قَالَ أَنَسُّ بن مالك "كَانَ رَسُولُ اللهِ صلى الله عليه وسلم مِنْ أَحْسَنِ النَّاسِ خُلُقًا
ما رأيتُ رجلًا الْتَقَمَ أُذُنَ رسولِ اللهِ صلى الله عليه وسلم ، فَيُنَحِّي رأسَه ، حتى يكونَ الرجلُ هو"
الذي يُنَحِّي رأسَه ، وما رأيتُ رجلًا أَخَذَ بيده فتَرَكَ يدَه ، حتى يكونَ الرجلُ هو الذي يَدَعُ يدَه ".

Anas ibn Malik related that the Messenger of Allah
(ﷺ) was always respectful and attentive: "If someone
whispered something in his ear, he would not turn his
head away until the other person withdrew. Similarly,
if someone grabbed his hand, he would not withdraw
it until the other person let go of his hand."

Sunan Abu Dawûd, hadith number 4794

قَالَ رَسُولُ اللهِ صَلَّى اللهُ عَلَيْهِ وَسَلَّمَ " إِذَا مَاتَ صَاحِبُكُمْ فَدَعُوهُ لاَ تَقَعُوا فِيهِ ".

The Messenger of Allah (ﷺ) said, "If your companion
dies, let him rest and do not speak ill of him."

Sunan Abu Dawûd, hadith number 4899

HADITHS ON PROPER BEHAVIOR

قَالَ رَسُولُ اللهِ صَلَّى اللَّهُ عَلَيْهِ وَسَلَّمَ " لاَ يَكُونُ اللَّعَّانُونَ شُفَعَاءَ وَلاَ شُهَدَاءَ يَوْمَ الْقِيَامَةِ ".

The Messenger of Allah (ﷺ) said, "Those who
habitually curse others will not be intercessors
or witnesses on the Day of Judgment."

Sahih Muslim, hadith number 2598 a

قَالَ رَسُولُ اللهِ صَلَّى اللَّهُ عَلَيْهِ وَسَلَّمَ " مَثَلُ الَّذِي يَتَصَدَّقُ بِالصَّدَقَةِ
ثُمَّ يَرْجِعُ فِيهَا كَمَثَلِ الْكَلْبِ قَاءَ ثُمَّ عَادَ فِي قَيْئِهِ فَأَكَلَهُ ".

The Messenger of Allah (ﷺ) said, "Whoever
gives a gift and then demands it back is like a
dog that returns to its vomit and eats it."

Sunan Al-Nasa'i, hadith number 3694

قَالَ رَسُولُ اللهِ صَلَّى اللهُ عَلَيْهِ وَسَلَّمَ " مَنْ أُعْطِيَ عَطَاءً فَوَجَدَ فَلْيَجْزِ بِهِ فَإِنْ
لَمْ يَجِدْ فَلْيُثْنِ بِهِ فَمَنْ أَثْنَى بِهِ فَقَدْ شَكَرَهُ وَمَنْ كَتَمَهُ فَقَدْ كَفَرَهُ".

The Prophet (ﷺ) said, "If someone is given something, he should
return the favor if he can afford it; if he cannot afford it, he
should praise the giver. Whoever praises him in return thanks
him, and whoever withholds praise is ungrateful to him."

Sunan Abu Dawûd, hadith number 4813

HADITHS ON PROPER BEHAVIOR

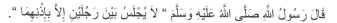

قَالَ رَسُولُ اللَّهِ صَلَّى اللَّهُ عَلَيْهِ وَسَلَّمَ " لَا يُجْلَسُ بَيْنَ رَجُلَيْنِ إِلاَّ بِإِذْنِهِمَا ".

The Messenger of Allah (ﷺ) said, "One should not sit between two people except with their permission."

Sunan Abu Dawûd, hadith number 4844

رُبَيِّعُ بِنْتِ مُعَوِّذِ ابْنِ عَفْرَاءَ قَالَتْ: " كُنَّا نَغْزُو مَعَ رَسُولِ اللَّهِ صَلَّى اللَّهُ عَلَيْهِ وَسَلَّمَ نَسْقِي الْقَوْمَ، وَنَخْدُمُهُمْ، وَنَرُدُّ الْقَتْلَى وَالْجَرْحَى إِلَى الْمَدِينَةِ ".

Rubai bint Mu'adh bin Afra related, "Together with the Messenger of Allah (ﷺ) we undertook military expeditions and supplied people with water, healed them and brought back to Medina the dead and wounded."

Sahih Al-Bukhari, hadith number 5679

قَالَ رَسُولُ اللَّهِ صَلَّى اللَّهُ عَلَيْهِ وَسَلَّمَ " إِذَا عَطَسَ أَحَدُكُمْ فَلْيَقُلِ الْحَمْدُ لِلَّهِ عَلَى كُلِّ حَالٍ وَلْيَقُلْ أَخُوهُ أَوْ صَاحِبُهُ يَرْحَمُكَ اللَّهُ وَيَقُولُ هُوَ يَهْدِيكُمُ اللَّهُ وَيُصْلِحُ بَالَكُمْ ".

The Messenger of Allah (ﷺ) said, "If one of you sneezes, he should say, 'Praise be to Allah in every situation,' and his brother or companion should say, 'May Allah have mercy on you!' And he should reply, "May Allah guide you and set your affairs in order."

Sunan Abu Dawûd, hadith number 5033

HADITHS ON PROPER BEHAVIOR

قَالَ رَسُولُ اللهِ صَلَّى اللهُ عَلَيْهِ وَسَلَّمَ "يُجْزِئُ عَنِ الْجَمَاعَةِ، إِذَا مَرُّوا أَنْ يُسَلِّمَ، أَحَدُهُمْ وَيُجْزِئُ عَنِ الْجُلُوسِ أَنْ يَرُدَّ أَحَدُهُمْ ".

The Messenger of Allah (ﷺ) said, "It suffices for the congregation, when they pass by people, that one of them gives the greeting, and it suffices for a sitting person that he responds to the greeting."

Sunan Abu Dawûd, hadith number 5210

[...] لاَ تَحْكُمْ بَيْنَ اثْنَيْنِ وَأَنْتَ غَضْبَانُ فَإِنِّي سَمِعْتُ رَسُولَ اللهِ صَلَّى اللهُ عَلَيْهِ وَسَلَّمَ يَقُولُ " لاَ يَحْكُمْ أَحَدٌ بَيْنَ اثْنَيْنِ وَهُوَ غَضْبَانُ".

"[...] Do not judge between two people when you are angry, for I heard Allah's Messenger (ﷺ) say, "Let none of you judge between two people when he is angry."

Sahih Muslim, hadith number 1717 a

سُئِلَ النَّبِيُّ صَلَّى اللهُ عَلَيْهِ وَسَلَّمَ أَيُّ الأَعْمَالِ أَحَبُّ إِلَى اللهِ قَالَ " أَدْوَمُهَا وَإِنْ قَلَّ ". وَقَالَ " اكْلَفُوا مِنَ الأَعْمَالِ مَا تُطِيقُونَ ".

The Prophet (ﷺ) was asked, "Which deeds are most beloved to Allah?" He said, "Regular and constant deeds, even if they are small." He added: "Do only those deeds which are within your capacity."

Sahih Al-Bukhari, hadith number 6465

HADITHS ON PROPER BEHAVIOR

عَنِ النَّبِيِّ صَلَّى اللهُ عَلَيْهِ وَسَلَّمَ فِيمَا يَرْوِي عَنْ رَبِّهِ عَزَّ وَجَلَّ قَالَ " إِنَّ اللهَ كَتَبَ الْحَسَنَاتِ
وَالسَّيِّئَاتِ، ثُمَّ بَيَّنَ ذَلِكَ فَمَنْ هَمَّ بِحَسَنَةٍ فَلَمْ يَعْمَلْهَا كَتَبَهَا اللهُ لَهُ عِنْدَهُ حَسَنَةً كَامِلَةً، فَإِنْ هُوَ هَمَّ بِهَا
فَعَمِلَهَا كَتَبَهَا اللهُ لَهُ عِنْدَهُ عَشْرَ حَسَنَاتٍ إِلَى سَبْعِمِائَةِ ضِعْفٍ إِلَى أَضْعَافٍ كَثِيرَةٍ، وَمَنْ هَمَّ بِسَيِّئَةٍ
فَلَمْ يَعْمَلْهَا كَتَبَهَا اللهُ لَهُ عِنْدَهُ حَسَنَةً كَامِلَةً، فَإِنْ هُوَ هَمَّ بِهَا فَعَمِلَهَا كَتَبَهَا اللهُ لَهُ سَيِّئَةً وَاحِدَةً ".

The Prophet (ﷺ) narrated from his Lord and said, "Allah commanded (the angels) to write down good deeds and bad deeds. If a person intends to do a good deed and does not do it, Allah writes down for him a complete good deed; and if he intends to do a good deed and actually did it, Allah writes down for him from ten to seven hundred times the good deeds: And if a person intends to do a bad deed and does not do it, Allah will write down for him a complete good deed, and if he intends to do a bad deed and actually did it, then Allah will write down for him a bad deed."

Sahih Al-Bukhari, hadith number 6491

قَالَ رَسُولُ اللهِ صَلَّى اللهُ عَلَيْهِ وَسَلَّمَ " لاَ صَلاةَ بِحَضْرَةِ الطَّعَامِ
وَلاَ وَهُوَ يُدَافِعُهُ الأَخْبَثَانِ" (الغائط والبول).

The Messenger of Allah (ﷺ) said, "Prayer should not be performed while eating, not even at the time when you are fighting two evils (when you need to do your physiological needs)."

Sunan Abu Dawûd, hadith number 89

HADITHS ON PROPER BEHAVIOR

قَالَ رَسُولُ اللهِ صَلَّى اللهُ عَلَيْهِ وَسَلَّمَ " إِذَا تَثَاوَبَ أَحَدُكُمْ فَلْيُمْسِكْ بِيَدِهِ عَلَى فِيهِ فَإِنَّ الشَّيْطَانَ يَدْخُلُ ".

The Messenger of Allah (ﷺ) said, "When any one
of you yawns, let him close his mouth with his
hand, otherwise it is the devil who enters it."

Sahih Muslim, hadith number 2995 a

عَنْ أَبِي هُرَيْرَةَ، أَنَّ رَسُولَ اللهِ صَلَّى اللهُ عَلَيْهِ وَسَلَّمَ قَالَ " مَنْ كَانَ لَهُ شَعْرٌ فَلْيُكْرِمْهُ ".

Abu Huraira related, The Prophet (ﷺ) said,
"Whoever has hair let him take care of it."

Sunan Abu Dawûd, hadith number 4163

قَالَ رَسُولُ اللهِ صَلَّى اللهُ عَلَيْهِ وَسَلَّمَ "مَثَلُ الْمُؤْمِنِ الَّذِي يَقْرَأُ الْقُرْآنَ مَثَلُ الْأُتْرُجَّةِ طَعْمُهَا
طَيِّبٌ وَرِيحُهَا طَيِّبٌ وَمَثَلُ الْمُؤْمِنِ الَّذِي لَا يَقْرَأُ الْقُرْآنَ كَمَثَلِ التَّمْرَةِ طَعْمُهَا طَيِّبٌ وَلَا
رِيحَ لَهَا وَمَثَلُ الْمُنَافِقِ الَّذِي يَقْرَأُ الْقُرْآنَ كَمَثَلِ الرَّيْحَانَةِ (أَوْ عشبة أخرى) رِيحُهَا طَيِّبٌ
وَطَعْمُهَا مُرٌّ وَمَثَلُ الْمُنَافِقِ الَّذِي لَا يَقْرَأُ الْقُرْآنَ كَمَثَلِ الْحَنْظَلَةِ طَعْمُهَا مُرٌّ وَلَا رِيحَ لَهَا".

The Messenger of Allah (ﷺ) said, "A believer who recites the
Qur'an is like a citron that tastes good and smells good. A
believer who does not recite the Qur'an is like a date that tastes
good but does not smell good. A hypocrite who recites the
Qur'an is like basil (or any other herb) that smells good but
tastes bitter. And a hypocrite who does not recite the Qur'an
is like colocynth, which tastes bitter and is not fragrant."

Sunan Al-Nasa'i, hadith number 5038

HADITHS ON PROPER BEHAVIOR

قَالَ رَسُولُ اللَّهِ صَلَّى اللَّهُ عَلَيْهِ وَسَلَّمَ " إِنَّ اللَّهَ قِبَلَ وَجْهِ أَحَدِكُمْ إِذَا صَلَّى فَلاَ يَبْزُقْ بَيْنَ يَدَيْهِ."

The Messenger of Allah (ﷺ) said, "When one of
you prays, Allah, the Exalted, is in front of him.
Therefore, he should not spit in front of him."

Sunan Abu Dawûd, hadith number 479

قَالَ النَّبِيُّ صَلَّى اللَّهُ عَلَيْهِ وَسَلَّمَ " الأَرْضُ كُلُّهَا مَسْجِدٌ إِلاَّ الْحَمَّامَ وَالْمَقْبَرَةَ".

The Prophet (ﷺ) said, "The whole earth is a place of
prayer, except for public baths and cemeteries."

Sunan Abu Dawûd, hadith number 492

عَنْ عَبْدِ اللَّهِ بْنِ مُغَفَّلٍ، قَالَ " نَهَى رَسُولُ اللَّهِ صَلَّى اللَّهُ عَلَيْهِ وَسَلَّمَ عَنِ التَّرَجُّلِ إِلاَّ غِبًّا".

'Abdullah ibn Mugaffal reported, "The Messenger of Allah
(ﷺ) forbade combing one's hair except every other day."

Sunan Abu Dawûd, hadith number 4159

عَنْ عَبْدِ اللَّهِ، قَالَ " لَعَنَ رَسُولُ اللَّهِ صَلَّى اللَّهُ عَلَيْهِ وَسَلَّمَ
الْوَاصِلَةَ وَالْمُسْتَوْصِلَةَ وَالْوَاشِمَةَ وَالْمُسْتَوْشِمَةَ ".

Abd Allah reported, "The Messenger of Allah (ﷺ) cursed the
woman who adds false hair and the woman who asks for it, and
the woman who tattoos herself and the woman who asks for it."

Sunan Abu Dawûd, hadith number 4168

HADITHS ON SUCCESS IN LIFE

قَالَ رَسُولُ اللهِ صَلَّى اللهُ عَلَيْهِ وَسَلَّمَ " إِنَّ اللهَ لاَ يَنْظُرُ إِلَى صُوَرِكُمْ
وَأَمْوَالِكُمْ وَلَكِنْ يَنْظُرُ إِلَى قُلُوبِكُمْ وَأَعْمَالِكُمْ ".

The Messenger of Allah (ﷺ) said, "Allah does not look at your
faces or your wealth, but He looks at your heart and your deeds."

Sahih Muslim, hadith number 2564 c

قَالَ رَسُولُ اللهِ صَلَّى اللهُ عَلَيْهِ وَسَلَّمَ " لَيْسَ الْغِنَى عَنْ كَثْرَةِ الْعَرَضِ وَلَكِنَّ الْغِنَى غِنَى النَّفْسِ ".

The Messenger of Allah (ﷺ) said, "Wealth does not lie in
the abundance of goods, but wealth is that of the soul."

Sahih Muslim, hadith number 1051

قَالَ رَسُولُ اللهِ صَلَّى اللهُ عَلَيْهِ وَسَلَّمَ لِعَلِي رضي الله عنه: " فوَاللهِ لَأَنْ
يهدِيَ اللهُ بكَ رجُلًا واحِدًا خيرٌ لكَ مِن أَنْ يكونَ لكَ حُمْرُ النَّعَمِ".

The Prophet (ﷺ) said to Ali (may Allah be pleased with
him), "By Allah, if a person is guided by Allah through
you, it is better for you than a herd of red camels."

Riyad as-Salihin, hadith number 1379

HADITHS ON SUCCESS IN LIFE

قَالَ رَسُولُ اللَّهِ صَلَّى اللَّهُ عَلَيْهِ وَسَلَّمَ " لَأَنْ يَحْتَطِبَ أَحَدُكُمْ حُزْمَةً
عَلَى ظَهْرِهِ خَيْرٌ مِنْ أَنْ يَسْأَلَ أَحَدًا، فَيُعْطِيَهُ أَوْ يَمْنَعَهُ ".

The Messenger of Allah (ﷺ) said, "Surely, it is better for any of
you to cut a bundle of firewood and carry it on your back rather
than to ask someone who may or may not give him (wood)."

Sahih Al-Bukhari, hadith number 2074

قَالَ رَسُولُ اللَّهِ صَلَّى اللَّهُ عَلَيْهِ وَسَلَّمَ " لَيْسَ الْغِنَى عَنْ كَثْرَةِ الْعَرَضِ وَلَكِنَّ الْغِنَى غِنَى النَّفْسِ ".

The Messenger of Allah (ﷺ) said, "Wealth does not consist in
having many possessions, but in contentment of the soul."

Yam'a Al Tirmidhi, hadith number 2373.

قَالَ رَسُولُ اللَّهِ صَلَّى اللَّهُ عَلَيْهِ وَسَلَّمَ " مَا ذِئْبَانِ جَائِعَانِ أُرْسِلاَ فِي غَنَمٍ
بِأَفْسَدَ لَهَا مِنْ حِرْصِ الْمَرْءِ عَلَى الْمَالِ وَالشَّرَفِ لِدِينِهِ ".

The Messenger of Allah (ﷺ) said, "Two wolves mingling
freely among the sheep are no more harmful to them than
a man's desire for wealth and honor is to his religion."

Sahih Al Tirmidhi, hadith number 2376

HADITHS ON SUCCESS IN LIFE

قَالَ رَسُولُ اللهِ صَلَّى اللهُ عَلَيْهِ وَسَلَّمَ " يَتْبَعُ الْمَيِّتَ ثَلَاثَةٌ، فَيَرْجِعُ اثْنَانِ وَيَبْقَى مَعَهُ وَاحِدٌ، يَتْبَعُهُ أَهْلُهُ وَمَالُهُ وَعَمَلُهُ، فَيَرْجِعُ أَهْلُهُ وَمَالُهُ، وَيَبْقَى عَمَلُهُ ".

The Messenger of Allah (ﷺ) said, "A dead man who is taken to his grave is followed by three, two of whom return (after his burial) and one remains with him: his relatives, his property and his deeds follow him; the relatives and his property leave him, while his deeds remain with him."

Sahih Al-Bukhari, hadith number 6514

قَالَ رَسُولُ اللهِ صَلَّى اللهُ عَلَيْهِ وَسَلَّمَ " عَجَبًا لِأَمْرِ الْمُؤْمِنِ إِنَّ أَمْرَهُ كُلَّهُ خَيْرٌ وَلَيْسَ ذَاكَ لِأَحَدٍ إِلاَّ لِلْمُؤْمِنِ إِنْ أَصَابَتْهُ سَرَّاءُ شَكَرَ فَكَانَ خَيْرًا لَهُ وَإِنْ أَصَابَتْهُ ضَرَّاءُ صَبَرَ فَكَانَ خَيْرًا لَهُ " .

The Messenger of Allah (ﷺ) said, "Strange are the ways of a believer, for there is good in all his affairs, and this is not the case with anyone except a believer. When he feels joy, he gives thanks (to Allah), so there is good for him in it, and when he encounters hardship and bears it with patience, there is good for him in it."

Sahih Muslim, hadith number 2999

عَنْ أَبِي هُرَيْرَةَ ـ رضى الله عنه ـ عَنِ النَّبِيِّ صَلَّى اللهُ عَلَيْهِ وَسَلَّمَ قَالَ " إِذَا أَنْفَقَتِ الْمَرْأَةُ مِنْ كَسْبِ زَوْجِهَا عَنْ غَيْرِ أَمْرِهِ، فَلَهُ نِصْفُ أَجْرِهِ " .

Abu Huraira reported, "The Prophet (ﷺ) said, "If a woman donates from her husband's income for charity without his permission, he will receive half of her reward."

Sahih Al-Bukhari, hadith number 2066

HADITHS ON SUCCESS IN LIFE

[...] أَتَيْتُ صَفْوَانَ بْنَ عَسَّالٍ الْمُرَادِيَّ فَقَالَ مَا جَاءَ بِكَ قُلْتُ أَنْبِطُ الْعِلْمَ . قَالَ فَإِنِّي سَمِعْتُ رَسُولَ اللَّهِ ـ صلى الله عليه وسلم ـ يَقُولُ " مَا مِنْ خَارِجٍ خَرَجَ مِنْ بَيْتِهِ فِي طَلَبِ الْعِلْمِ إِلاَّ وَضَعَتْ لَهُ الْمَلاَئِكَةُ أَجْنِحَتَهَا رِضًا بِمَا يَصْنَعُ ".

[...] I went to Safwan bin 'Assal Al-Muradi and he asked me, 'What has brought you here?' ' I said, 'I am seeking knowledge.' He said, I heard the Messenger of Allah (ﷺ) say, "Whoever goes out of his house to seek knowledge, the angels lower their wings to approve his actions."'

Sunan Ibn Mayah, hadith number 226

سَمِعْتُ رَسُولَ اللَّهِ صَلَّى اللَّهُ عَلَيْهِ وَسَلَّمَ، يَقُولُ: " إِنَّمَا الأَعْمَالُ بِالنِّيَّاتِ، وَإِنَّمَا لِكُلِّ امْرِئٍ مَا نَوَى [...]".

I heard the Messenger of Allah (ﷺ) say, "The reward of actions depends on intentions. Everyone gets the reward of what he has intended. [...]"

Sahih Al-Bukhari, hadith number 1

قَالَ رَسُولُ اللَّهِ ـ صَلَّى اللَّهُ عَلَيْهِ وَسَلَّمَ ـ " ذَرُونِي مَا تَرَكْتُكُمْ فَإِنَّمَا هَلَكَ مَنْ كَانَ قَبْلَكُمْ بِسُؤَالِهِمْ وَاخْتِلاَفِهِمْ عَلَى أَنْبِيَائِهِمْ فَإِذَا أَمَرْتُكُمْ بِشَيْءٍ فَخُذُوا مِنْهُ مَا اسْتَطَعْتُمْ وَإِذَا نَهَيْتُكُمْ عَنْ شَيْءٍ فَانْتَهُوا ".

The Messenger of Allah (ﷺ) said, "Leave me as I leave you (do not ask about trivial matters about which I have deliberately told you nothing). For those who came before you perished because of their many questions and disagreements with their prophets. If I have commanded you to do something, do it to the best of your ability. And if I have forbidden you to do anything, do not do it".

Sunan Ibn Mayah, hadith number 2

HADITHS ON SUCCESS IN LIFE

[...] فَقَالَ رَسُولُ اللَّهِ صَلَّى اللَّهُ عَلَيْهِ وَسَلَّمَ " مَنْ دَلَّ عَلَى خَيْرٍ فَلَهُ مِثْلُ أَجْرِ فَاعِلِهِ " .

[...] Then the Messenger of Allah (ﷺ) said, "If anyone guides another to perform a good deed, he will receive the same reward as the one who performs it."

Sunan Abu Dawûd, hadith number 5129

قَالَ رَسُولُ اللَّهِ صَلَّى اللَّهُ عَلَيْهِ وَسَلَّمَ " مَنْ عَلَّمَ عِلْمًا فَلَهُ أَجْرُ
مَنْ عَمِلَ بِهِ لاَ يَنْقُصُ مِنْ أَجْرِ الْعَامِلِ " .

The Prophet (ﷺ) said, "Whoever teaches knowledge will have the reward of one who acts accordingly, without diminishing his reward in the least."

Sunan Ibn Mayah, Hadith number 240

قَالَ رَسُولُ اللَّهِ صَلَّى اللَّهُ عَلَيْهِ وَسَلَّمَ " مَا مِنْ رَجُلٍ يَسْلُكُ طَرِيقًا يَطْلُبُ فِيهِ عِلْمًا
إِلاَّ سَهَّلَ اللَّهُ لَهُ بِهِ طَرِيقَ الْجَنَّةِ وَمَنْ أَبْطَأَ بِهِ عَمَلُهُ لَمْ يُسْرِعْ بِهِ نَسَبُهُ " .

The Messenger of Allah (ﷺ) said, "If a person travels a path in search of knowledge, Allah will ease his way to Paradise, and whoever becomes sluggish by his deeds will be not hastened by his lineage."

Sunan Abu Dawûd, hadith number 3643

HADITHS ON WELFARE

ايْمُ اللَّهِ لَقَدْ سَمِعْتُ رَسُولَ اللَّهِ صَلَّى اللَّهُ عَلَيْهِ وَسَلَّمَ يَقُولُ " إِنَّ السَّعِيدَ لَمَنْ جُنِّبَ الْفِتَنَ إِنَّ السَّعِيدَ لَمَنْ جُنِّبَ الْفِتَنَ إِنَّ السَّعِيدَ لَمَنْ جُنِّبَ الْفِتَنَ وَلَمَنِ ابْتُلِيَ فَصَبَرَ فَوَاهًا " .

I swear by Allah that I heard the Messenger of Allah (ﷺ)
say, "Happy is he who avoids temptations; happy is he who
avoids temptations; happy is he who avoids temptations; but
how beautiful is he who is afflicted and remains patient."

Sunan Abu Dawûd, hadith number 4263

قَالَ رَسُولُ اللَّهِ صَلَّى اللَّهُ عَلَيْهِ وَسَلَّمَ " لَيْسَ الْغِنَى عَنْ كَثْرَةِ الْعَرَضِ، وَلَكِنَّ الْغِنَى غِنَى النَّفْسِ " .

The Prophet (ﷺ) said, "Wealth does not consist
in having many possessions, but true wealth
is the feeling of sufficiency in the soul."

Sahih Al-Bukhari, hadith number 6446

عَنْ أَبِي هُرَيْرَةَ، قَالَ ـ وَلاَ أَعْلَمُهُ إِلاَّ قَدْ رَفَعَهُ ـ قَالَ رَسُولُ اللَّهِ صَلَّى اللَّهُ عَلَيْهِ وَسَلَّمَ " يَقُولُ اللَّهُ سُبْحَانَهُ يَا ابْنَ آدَمَ تَفَرَّغْ لِعِبَادَتِي أَمْلأْ صَدْرَكَ غِنًى وَأَسُدَّ فَقْرَكَ وَإِنْ لَمْ تَفْعَلْ مَلأْتُ صَدْرَكَ شُغْلاً وَلَمْ أَسُدَّ فَقْرَكَ " .

Abu Huraira said, "I do not know, except that he attributed it
to the Prophet (ﷺ)" - "Allah says, 'O son of Adam, free yourself
for My worship, and I will fill your heart with contentment and
relieve your poverty. But if you do not do so, I will fill your heart
with preoccupations and leave your poverty unabated.'"

Sunan Ibn Mayah, hadith number 4107

HADITHS ON WELFARE

قَالَ رَسُولُ اللَّهِ صَلَّى اللَّهُ عَلَيْهِ وَسَلَّمَ " قَدْ أَفْلَحَ مَنْ هُدِيَ إِلَى الْإِسْلَامِ وَرُزِقَ الْكَفَافَ وَقَنِعَ بِهِ ".

The Messenger of Allah (ﷺ) said, "He has indeed succeeded who has been guided to Islam, granted sufficiency, and is content with it."

Sunan Ibn Mayah, hadith number 4138

جَاءَ رجلٌ إلى النبي صَلَّى اللَّهُ عَلَيْهِ وَسَلَّمَ فقال: يا رسول الله دلني على عملٍ إذا عملته أحبني الله، واحبني الناسُ، فقَالَ: " ازهد في الدنيا يحبكُ اللهُ، وازهد فيما عند الناسِ يحبكُ الناسُ ".

A man came to the Prophet (ﷺ) and said, "O Messenger of Allah, what should I do so that Allah and the people will love me?" He (ﷺ) said, "Have no desire for this world, and Allah will love you; and have no desire for what people possess, and people will love you."

Riyad as-Salihin, hadith number 471

قَالَ رَسُولُ اللَّهِ صَلَّى اللَّهُ عَلَيْهِ وَسَلَّمَ " مَنْ يُحْرَمِ الرِّفْقَ يُحْرَمِ الْخَيْرَ ".

The Messenger of Allah (ﷺ) said, "Whoever is deprived of kindness is deprived of goodness."

Sahih Muslim, hadith number 2592 a

ḤADITHS ON WELFARE

قَالَ رَسُولُ اللهِ صَلَّى اللهُ عَلَيْهِ وَسَلَّمَ " [...] سَلُوا اللَّهَ الْعَفْوَ وَالْعَافِيَةَ
فَإِنَّ أَحَدًا لَمْ يُعْطَ بَعْدَ الْيَقِينِ خَيْرًا مِنَ الْعَافِيَةِ ".

The Messenger of Allah (ﷺ) said: [...] "Ask Allah for
pardon and well-being, for after certainty, no one
is given anything better than well-being."

Sahih Al Tirmidhi, Hadith number 3558

HADITHS ON THE WELFARE OF OTHERS

قَالَ رَسُولُ اللهِ صَلَّى اللهُ عَلَيْهِ وَسَلَّمَ " إِذَا كُنْتُمْ ثَلَاثَةً فَلَا يَتَنَاجَى
اثْنَانِ دُونَ صَاحِبِهِمَا فَإِنَّ ذَلِكَ يُحْزِنُهُ " .

The Messenger of Allah (ﷺ) said, "When there are three of you, two should not converse privately to the exclusion of the third, for that may grieve him."

Sunan Ibn Mayah, hadith number 3775

عَنْ سَهْلِ بنِ سعد، أَنَّ النَّبِيَّ صَلَّى اللهُ عَلَيْهِ وَسَلَّمَ قَالَ " أَنَا وَكَافِلُ الْيَتِيمِ كَهَاتَيْنِ في الْجَنَّةِ " .
وَقَرَنَ بَيْنَ أَصْبُعَيْهِ الْوُسْطَى وَالَّتِي تَلِي الإِبْهَامَ (لإِظْهَارِ مَدَى قربهما من بعضهما البعض) .

Sahl ibn Saad related that the Prophet (ﷺ) said, "I and the one who takes care of an orphan will be like this in Paradise" and he put his middle and index finger together (to show how close they would be).

Sunan Abu Dawûd, hadith number 5150

قَالَ النَّبِيّ صَلَّى اللهُ عَلَيْهِ وَسَلَّمَ " السَّاعِي عَلَى الأَرْمَلَةِ وَالْمِسْكِينِ كَالْمُجَاهِدِ
فِي سَبِيلِ اللهِ. [...] وَكَالْقَائِمِ لاَ يَفْتُرُ وَكَالصَّائِمِ لاَ يُفْطِرُ " .

The Prophet (ﷺ) said, "Whoever strives to help a widow and a needy person is like one who strives for the cause of Allah. [...] He is like one who constantly attends prayer and observes the fast without breaking it.

Sahih Muslim, hadith number 2982

HADITHS ON THE
WELFARE OF OTHERS

قَالَ رَسُولُ اللهِ صَلَّى اللهُ عَلَيْهِ وَسَلَّمَ " مَنْ عَادَ مَرِيضًا لَمْ يَزَلْ فِي خُرْفَةِ الْجَنَّةِ حَتَّى يَرْجِعَ " .

The Messenger of Allah (ﷺ) said, "Whoever visits the sick is like one who stays in the garden of paradise until he leaves."

Sahih Muslim, hadith number 2568

HADITHS ON THE FORMATION OF GOOD CHARACTER

"[...] يا رسول الله، قل لي قولاً وأقللْ عليَّ لعلي أعقله قال: " لا تغضب. [...] فأعدت عليه مراراً، كل ذلك يقول: لا تغضب" .

O Messenger of Allah, teach me something that is not too much for me, so that perhaps I can stick to it. He said to me, "Do not be angry. I asked him again and again and each time he said, "Do not be angry."

Sahih al-Bukhari, hadith number 6116

قَالَ رَسُولُ اللهِ صَلَّى اللهُ عَلَيْهِ وَسَلَّم " التأنّي من الله والعجلة من الشيطان ".

The Messenger of Allah (ﷺ) said, "Prudence comes from Allah, and haste comes from Ash-Shaitan."

Yam'a Al Tirmidhi, hadith number 2012.

قَالَ رَسُولُ اللهِ صَلَّى اللهُ عَلَيْهِ وَسَلَّمَ " لَيْسَ الشَّدِيدُ بِالصُّرَعَةِ، إِنَّمَا الشَّدِيدُ الَّذِي يَمْلِكُ نَفْسَهُ عِنْدَ الْغَضَبِ ".

The Messenger of Allah (ﷺ) said, "The strong person is not the one who wrestles others down. Rather, the strong person is the one who controls himself when he is angry."

Sahih Al-Bukhari, hadith number 6114

HADITHS ON THE FORMATION OF GOOD CHARACTER

قَالَ النَّبِيِّ صَلَّى اللهُ عَلَيْهِ وَسَلَّمَ " إِنَّ أَبْغَضَ الرِّجَالِ إِلَى اللهِ الْأَلَدُّ الْخَصِمُ ".

The Prophet (ﷺ) said, "The most hated of people to Allah is the one who is most quarrelsome and argumentative."

Sahih Al-Bukhari, hadith number 2457

نَاسُ مِنَ الْأَنْصَارِ سَأَلُوا رَسُولَ اللهِ صلى الله عليه وسلم فَأَعْطَاهُمْ، ثُمَّ سَأَلُوهُ فَأَعْطَاهُمْ، حَتَّى نَفِدَ مَا عِنْدَهُ فَقَالَ " مَا يَكُونُ عِنْدِي مِنْ خَيْرٍ فَلَنْ أَدَّخِرَهُ عَنْكُمْ، وَمَنْ يَسْتَعْفِفْ يُعِفَّهُ اللهُ، وَمَنْ يَسْتَغْنِ يُغْنِهِ اللهُ، وَمَنْ يَتَصَبَّرْ يُصَبِّرْهُ اللهُ، وَمَا أُعْطِيَ أَحَدٌ عَطَاءً خَيْرًا وَأَوْسَعَ مِنَ الصَّبْرِ ".

Some Ansari asked the Messenger of Allah (ﷺ) for something and he gave it to them. They asked him again for something and he gave it to them again. And then they asked him and he again gave it to them until all that he had was finished. And then he said, "If I had anything, I would not withhold it from you. Whoever refrains from asking others, Allah will satisfy him, and whoever tries to provide for himself, Allah will provide for him. And whoever remains patient, Allah will make him patient. To none can be granted a better and greater blessing than patience."

Sahih Al-Bukhari, hadith number 1469

قَالَ رَسُولُ اللهِ صَلَّى اللهُ عَلَيْهِ وَسَلَّمَ " [...] وَلَنْ تُعْطَوْا عَطَاءً خَيْرًا وَأَوْسَعَ مِنَ الصَّبْرِ ".

The Messenger of Allah (ﷺ) said, " [...] You will not be given a gift better and more comprehensive than patience."

Sahih al-Bukhari, hadith number 6470

HADITHS ON THE FORMATION OF GOOD CHARACTER

قَالَ رَسُولُ اللَّهِ صَلَّى اللَّهُ عَلَيْهِ وَسَلَّمَ " إِنَّ مِمَّا أَدْرَكَ النَّاسُ مِنْ كَلَامِ النُّبُوَّةِ الْأُولَى إِذَا لَمْ تَسْتَحِ فَاصْنَعْ مَا شِئْتَ " .

The Messenger of Allah (ﷺ) said, "Among the words that people have learned from the previous prophets are, 'If you feel no shame, do whatever you want.'"

Sunan Ibn Mayah, hadith number 4183

قَالَ رَسُولُ اللَّهِ صَلَّى اللَّهُ عَلَيْهِ وَسَلَّمَ " مَنْ كَظَمَ غَيْظًا وَهُوَ قَادِرٌ عَلَى أَنْ يُنْفِذَهُ دَعَاهُ اللَّهُ عَلَى رُءُوسِ الْخَلَائِقِ يَوْمَ الْقِيَامَةِ حَتَّى يُخَيِّرَهُ فِي أَيِّ الْحُورِ شَاءَ " .

The Messenger of Allah (ﷺ) said, "Whoever restrains his anger when he can unleash it, Allah will call him before all creation on the Day of Resurrection and give him any houri (virgins in Paradise) to choose from."

Sunan Ibn Mayah, hadith number 4186

جَاءَ رَجُلٌ إِلَى النَّبِيِّ ـ صَلَّى اللَّهُ عَلَيْهِ وَسَلَّمَ ـ فَقَالَ يَا رَسُولَ اللَّهِ عَلِّمْنِي وَأَوْجِزْ . قَالَ " إِذَا قُمْتَ فِي صَلَاتِكَ فَصَلِّ صَلَاةَ مُوَدِّعٍ وَلاَ تَكَلَّمْ بِكَلَامٍ تَعْتَذِرُ مِنْهُ وَأَجْمِعِ الْيَأْسَ عَمَّا فِي أَيْدِي النَّاسِ " .

A man came to the Prophet (ﷺ) and said, "O Messenger of Allah, teach me, but keep it brief and to the point.' ' He said to him, 'When you get up to pray, pray like a man in his last day. Say nothing for which you have to apologize. And give up expecting what others have."

Sunan Ibn Mayah, hadith number 4171

HADITHS ON THE FORMATION
OF GOOD CHARACTER

قَالَ رَسُولُ اللهِ صَلَّى اللهُ عَلَيْهِ وَسَلَّمَ وَهُوَ يَذْكُرُ الصَّدَقَةَ وَالتَّعَفُّفَ عَنِ الْمَسْأَلَةِ الْيَدُ
"الْعُلْيَا خَيْرٌ مِنَ الْيَدِ السُّفْلَى وَالْيَدُ الْعُلْيَا الْمُنْفِقَةُ وَالْيَدُ السُّفْلَى السَّائِلَةُ " .

The Messenger of Allah (ﷺ) said in speaking of charity
and those who do not ask for it "The higher hand is
better than the lower hand; the higher hand is the one
that gives and the lower hand is the one that asks."

Sunan Al-Nassai, hadith number 2533

قَالَ رَسُولُ اللهِ صَلَّى اللهُ عَلَيْهِ وَسَلَّمَ " إِنَّ اللهَ تَعَالى أَوْحَى إِلَيَّ أَنْ تَوَاضَعُوا
حَتَّى لاَ يَبْغِيَ أَحَدٌ على أَحَدٍ ولا يفخرُ أَحَدٌ على أَحَدٍ" .

The Messenger of Allah (ﷺ) said, "Allah, the Most High,
has revealed to me that you should be humble so that
no one will transgress or boast before another."

Sahih Muslim, hadith number 2865

قَالَ رَسُولُ اللهِ صَلَّى اللهُ عَلَيْهِ وَسَلَّمَ " الرَّاحِمُونَ يَرْحَمُهُمُ الرَّحْمَنُ
ارْحَمُوا أَهْلَ الأَرْضِ يَرْحَمْكُمْ مَنْ فِي السَّمَاءِ " .

The Prophet (ﷺ) said: "The Merciful has mercy on those
who are merciful. If you have mercy on those on earth,
He who is in heaven will have mercy on you. "

Sunan Abu Dawûd, hadith number 4941

HADITHS ON THE FORMATION
OF GOOD CHARACTER

قَالَ لِي رَسُولُ اَللَّهِ صَلَّى اللَّهُ عَلَيْهِ وَسَلَّمَ " قُلِ اَلْحَقَّ، وَلَوْ كَانَ مُرًّا ".

The Messenger of Allah (ﷺ) said, "Speak
the truth even if it is bitter."

Bulugh Al Maram, hadith number 132

قَالَ رَسُولُ اللَّهِ صَلَّى اللَّهُ عَلَيْهِ وَسَلَّمَ " لاَ تُكْثِرُوا الضَّحِكَ فَإِنَّ كَثْرَةَ الضَّحِكِ تُمِيتُ الْقَلْبَ ".

The Messenger of Allah (ﷺ) said, "Do not laugh too
much, for too much laughter kills the heart."

Sunan Ibn Mayah, hadith number 4193

عَنِ النَّبِيِّ صَلَّى اللَّهُ عَلَيْهِ وَسَلَّمَ قَالَ " قَالَ اللَّهُ تَعَالَى ثَلاَثَةٌ أَنَا خَصْمُهُمْ يَوْمَ الْقِيَامَةِ رَجُلٌ أَعْطَى
بِي ثُمَّ غَدَرَ، وَرَجُلٌ بَاعَ حُرًّا فَأَكَلَ ثَمَنَهُ، وَرَجُلٌ اسْتَأْجَرَ أَجِيرًا فَاسْتَوْفَى مِنْهُ وَلَمْ يُعْطِهِ أَجْرَهُ ".

The Prophet (ﷺ) narrated, "Allah, the Exalted, has said:
'I will be the opponent of three persons on the Day of
Resurrection: a man who gives something in charity and then
shows it off, a man who sells a free person and consumes
the price, and a man who hires someone and receives
full work from him but does not pay him his wages.'"

Sahih Al-Bukhari, hadith number 2270

HADITHS ON THE FORMATION
OF GOOD CHARACTER

قَالَ رَسُولُ اللهِ صَلَّى اللهُ عَلَيْهِ وَسَلَّمَ " لَا حَسَدَ إِلاَّ فِي اثْنَتَيْنِ، رَجُلٌ آتَاهُ اللهُ مَالاً فَسَلَّطَهُ عَلَى هَلَكَتِهِ فِي الْحَقِّ، وَآخَرُ آتَاهُ اللهُ حِكْمَةً فَهُوَ يَقْضِي بِهَا وَيُعَلِّمُهَا " .

The Messenger of Allah (ﷺ) said, "Do not desire to be like anyone except in two cases: (1) A man to whom Allah has given wealth and he spends it righteously. (2) A man to whom Allah has given wisdom and he acts upon it and teaches it to others."

Sahih Al-Bukhari, hadith number 7141

قَالَ رَسُولُ اللهِ صَلَّى اللهُ عَلَيْهِ وَسَلَّمَ " لَا حَسَدَ إِلاَّ فِي اثْنَتَيْنِ رَجُلٌ آتَاهُ اللهُ الْقُرْآنَ فَهُوَ يَقُومُ بِهِ آنَاءَ اللَّيْلِ وَآنَاءَ النَّهَارِ وَرَجُلٌ آتَاهُ اللهُ مَالاً فَهُوَ يُنْفِقُهُ آنَاءَ اللَّيْلِ وَآنَاءَ النَّهَارِ " .

The Messenger of Allah (ﷺ) said, "There is no envy except in two cases. A man to whom Allah has given the Qur'an to recite it day and night, and a man to whom Allah has given wealth to spend it day and night for the good."

Sunan Ibn Mayah, hadith number 4209

قَالَ رَسُولُ اللهِ صَلَّى اللهُ عَلَيْهِ وَسَلَّمَ " [...] إِنَّ مِنْ خِيَارِكُمْ أَحْسَنَكُمْ أَخْلَاقًا " .

The Messenger of Allah (ﷺ) said, " [...] The best among you are those who have the best manners and the best character."

Sahih Al-Bukhari, hadith number 3559

HADITHS ON THE FORMATION
OF GOOD CHARACTER

قَالَ رَسُولُ اللهِ صَلَّى اللهُ عَلَيْهِ وَسَلَّمَ " إِنَّ اللهَ أَوْحَى إِلَيَّ أَنْ تَوَاضَعُوا حَتَّى لاَ يَبْغِيَ أَحَدٌ عَلَى أَحَدٍ وَلاَ يَفْخَرَ أَحَدٌ عَلَى أَحَدٍ " .

The Prophet (ﷺ) said, "Allah has revealed to me that you should be humble so that no one shows pride over another, and no one oppresses another."

Sunan Abu Dawûd, hadith number 4895

قَالَ رَسُولُ اللهِ صَلَّى اللهُ عَلَيْهِ وَسَلَّمَ " إِنَّ اللهَ رَفِيقٌ يُحِبُّ الرِّفْقَ، وَيُعْطِي عَلَيْهِ مَا لاَ يُعْطِي عَلَى الْعُنْفِ".

The Messenger of Allah (ﷺ) said, "Allah is Gentle and loves gentleness. He gives due to gentleness that which He does not give to harshness."

Al Adab Al Mufrad, hadith number 472

قَالَ رَسُولُ اللهِ صَلَّى اللهُ عَلَيْهِ وَسَلَّمَ " إن اللهَ ليرضىَ عن العبد أن يأكلَ الأكلةَ، فيحمَده عَليها، أو يشربَ الشربةَ، فيحمَده عَليها ".

The Messenger of Allah (ﷺ) said, "Allah is pleased with His servant who eats a meal and praises Him for it, and who drinks and praises Him for it."

Riyad as-Salihin, hadith number 436

HADITHS ON THE FORMATION OF GOOD CHARACTER

قَالَ رَسُولُ اللهِ صَلَّى اللهُ عَلَيْهِ وَسَلَّمَ " يَا عَائِشَةُ إِنَّ اللهَ رَفِيقٌ يُحِبُّ الرِّفْقَ وَيُعْطِي عَلَى الرِّفْقِ مَا لاَ يُعْطِي عَلَى الْعُنْفِ وَمَا لاَ يُعْطِي عَلَى مَا سِوَاهُ ".

The Messenger of Allah (ﷺ) said, "Aisha! Allah is Gentle and loves gentleness. He gives due to gentleness that which He does not give to harshness, and does not grant anything other than it (gentleness)."

Sahih Muslim, hadith number 2593

قَالَ رَسُولُ اللهِ صَلَّى اللهُ عَلَيْهِ وَسَلَّمَ " إِذَا نَظَرَ أَحَدُكُمْ إِلَى مَنْ فُضِّلَ عَلَيْهِ فِي الْمَالِ وَالْخَلْقِ، فَلْيَنْظُرْ إِلَى مَنْ هُوَ أَسْفَلَ مِنْهُ ".

The Messenger of Allah (ﷺ) said, "If one of you looks at a person who is superior to him in possessions and (good) appearance, then let him also look at one who is inferior to him."

Sahih Al-Bukhari, hadith number 6490

قَالَ رَسُولُ اللهِ صَلَّى اللهُ عَلَيْهِ وَسَلَّمَ " بَادِرُوا بِالأَعْمَالِ فِتَنًا كَقِطَعِ اللَّيْلِ الْمُظْلِمِ يُصْبِحُ الرَّجُلُ مُؤْمِنًا وَيُمْسِي كَافِرًا أَوْ يُمْسِي مُؤْمِنًا وَيُصْبِحُ كَافِرًا يَبِيعُ دِينَهُ بِعَرَضٍ مِنَ الدُّنْيَا ".

The Messenger of Allah (ﷺ) said, "Hasten to perform good deeds before there emerges trials like pieces of a dark night, where a person wakes up as a believer and by evening becomes a disbeliever, or in the evening becomes a believer and wakes up as a disbeliever. He sells his religion for a trivial worldly gain."

Riyad as-Salihin, hadith number 87

HADITHS ON THE FORMATION OF GOOD CHARACTER

قَالَ رَسُولُ اللهِ صَلَّى اللهُ عَلَيْهِ وَسَلَّمَ " مَا نَقَصَتْ صَدَقَةٌ مِنْ مَالٍ وَمَا زَادَ اللهُ عَبْدًا بِعَفْوٍ إِلَّا عِزًّا وَمَا تَوَاضَعَ أَحَدٌ لِلَّهِ إِلَّا رَفَعَهُ اللهُ".

The Messenger of Allah (ﷺ) said, "Charity does not diminish wealth. Whoever forgives others, Allah increases his honor; and whoever humbles himself for the sake of Allah, Allah increases his status."

Sahih Muslim, hadith number 2588

قَالَ رَسُولُ اللهِ صَلَّى اللهُ عَلَيْهِ وَسَلَّمَ " كُلُّ بَنِي آدَمَ خَطَّاءٌ وَخَيْرُ الْخَطَّائِينَ التَّوَّابُونَ " .

The Messenger of Allah (ﷺ) said, "All the children of Adam are prone to making mistakes, and the best of those who make mistakes are those who repent."

Sunan Ibn Mayah, hadith number 4251

قَالَ رَسُولُ اللهِ صَلَّى اللهُ عَلَيْهِ وَسَلَّمَ " إِنَّ الْمُؤْمِنَ لَيُدْرِكُ بِحُسْنِ خُلُقِهِ دَرَجَةَ الصَّائِمِ الْقَائِمِ " .

The Messenger of Allah (ﷺ) said: "By his good character, a believer will reach the level of a person who prays at night and fasts during the day. "

Sunan Abu Dawûd, hadith number 4798

HADITHS ON SAFETY AND SECURITY

عَنْ أَبِي، هُرَيْرَةَ أَنَّ النَّبِيَّ صَلَّى اللهُ عَلَيْهِ وَسَلَّمَ قَالَ " إِذَا سَمِعْتُمْ صِيَاحَ الدِّيَكَةِ فَاسْأَلُوا اللهَ مِنْ فَضْلِهِ فَإِنَّهَا رَأَتْ مَلَكًا وَإِذَا سَمِعْتُمْ نَهِيقَ الْحِمَارِ فَتَعَوَّذُوا بِاللهِ مِنَ الشَّيْطَانِ فَإِنَّهَا رَأَتْ شَيْطَانًا "

Abu Huraira related that the Messenger of Allah (ﷺ) said, "When you hear the crowing of the rooster, ask Allah for His favor, for it has seen the angels, and when you hear the ass's paw, seek refuge in Allah from Satan, for it has seen Satan."

Sahih Muslim, hadith number 2729

قَالَ النَّبِيُّ صَلَّى اللهُ عَلَيْهِ وَسَلَّمَ " لاَ تَكْذِبُوا عَلَيَّ، فَإِنَّهُ مَنْ كَذَبَ عَلَيَّ فَلْيَلِجِ النَّارَ ".

The Prophet (ﷺ) said, "Do not lie against me, for whoever lies against me deliberately, let him take his place in the Hellfire."

Sahih Al-Bukhari, hadith number 106

قَالَ رَسُولُ اللهِ صَلَّى اللهُ عَلَيْهِ وَسَلَّمَ " لاَ تَتَمَنَّوُا الْمَوْتَ ".

The Messenger of Allah (ﷺ) said, "Do not wish for death."

Sahih Al-Bukhari, hadith number 7233

HADITHS ON SAFETY AND SECURITY

قَالَ رَسُولُ اللَّهِ صَلَّى اللَّهُ عَلَيْهِ وَسَلَّمَ " لاَ تَكْذِبُوا عَلَىَّ فَإِنَّ الْكَذِبَ عَلَىَّ يُولِجُ النَّارَ " .

The Messenger of Allah (ﷺ) said, "Do not tell lies about me, for telling lies about me leads to Hellfire."

Sunan Ibn Mayah, hadith number 31

[...] سَمِعْتُ النَّبِيَّ صَلَّى اللَّهُ عَلَيْهِ وَسَلَّمَ يَقُولُ " الرُّؤْيَا مِنَ اللَّهِ، وَالْحُلْمُ مِنَ الشَّيْطَانِ، فَإِذَا رَأَى أَحَدُكُمْ شَيْئًا يَكْرَهُهُ فَلْيَنْفِثْ حِينَ يَسْتَيْقِظُ ثَلاَثَ مَرَّاتٍ وَيَتَعَوَّذْ مِنْ شَرِّهَا، فَإِنَّهَا لاَ تَضُرُّهُ " .

I heard the Prophet (ﷺ) saying, "Dreams are from Allah, and nightmares are from Satan. So, if any of you sees something he dislikes in a dream, let him blow three times when he wakes up and seek refuge in Allah from its evil, for it will not harm him."

Sahih Al-Bukhari, hadith number 5747

جَاءَتْ فَأْرَةٌ فَأَخَذَتْ تَجُرُّ الْفَتِيلَةَ فَجَاءَتْ بِهَا فَأَلْقَتْهَا بَيْنَ يَدَىْ رَسُولِ اللَّهِ صَلَّى اللَّهُ عَلَيْهِ وَسَلَّمَ عَلَى الْخُمْرَةِ الَّتِي كَانَ قَاعِدًا عَلَيْهَا فَأَحْرَقَتْ مِنْهَا مِثْلَ مَوْضِعِ الدِّرْهَمِ فَقَالَ " إِذَا نِمْتُمْ فَأَطْفِئُوا سُرُجَكُمْ فَإِنَّ الشَّيْطَانَ يَدُلُّ مِثْلَ هَذِهِ عَلَى هَذَا فَتُحْرِقَكُمْ " .

A mouse came and started pulling a lighted wick. It came with it and threw it in front of the Prophet (ﷺ), who was sitting on the mat. It burned a part of the mat equal to the space of a dirham. He said, "When you go to bed, extinguish your lamps, for the Satan guides like this mouse for this wick and sets the house on fire."

Sunan Abu Dawûd, hadith number 5247

HADITHS ON SAFETY AND SECURITY

قَالَ رَسُولُ اللهِ صَلَّى اللهُ عَلَيْهِ وَسَلَّمَ " مَنْ قَرَأَ بِالآيَتَيْنِ مِنْ آخِرِ سُورَةِ الْبَقَرَةِ فِي لَيْلَةٍ كَفَتَاهُ".

The Prophet (ﷺ) said, "If someone recites the
last two verses of Surat Al-Baqara at night, that
is sufficient for him (as protection)."

Sahih Al-Bukhari, hadith number 5009

قَالَ رَسُولُ اللهِ صَلَّى اللهُ عَلَيْهِ وَسَلَّمَ " لَا تُرْسِلُوا فَوَاشِيَكُمْ – أي كل ما ينتشر
من ماشية وغيرها - وَصِبْيَانَكُمْ إِذَا غَابَتِ الشَّمْسُ حَتَّى تَذْهَبَ فَحْمَةُ الْعِشَاءِ ،
فَإِنَّ الشَّيَاطِينَ تَنْبَعِثُ إِذَا غَابَتِ الشَّمْسُ حَتَّى تَذْهَبَ فَحْمَةُ الْعِشَاءِ ".

The Messenger of Allah(ﷺ) said, "Do not send forth your cattle
and your children when the sun has set until the darkness of the
evening is intense, for indeed, the devils are scattered abroad
when the sun sets until the darkness of the evening is intense."

Sahih Muslim, hadith number 2013 a

قَالَ رَسُولُ اللهِ صَلَّى اللهُ عَلَيْهِ وَسَلَّمَ " الرُّؤْيَا مِنَ اللهِ، وَالْحُلُمُ مِنَ الشَّيْطَانِ ".

The Prophet (ﷺ) said, "A good true dream is from
Allah, and a bad dream is from Satan."

Sahih Al-Bukhari, hadith number 6984

HADITHS ON SAFETY AND SECURITY

قَالَ رَسُولُ اللهِ صَلَّى اللهُ عَلَيْهِ وَسَلَّمَ " لاَ تَتْرُكُوا النَّارَ فِي بُيُوتِكُمْ حِينَ تَنَامُونَ ".

The Prophet (ﷺ) said, "Do not leave the fire burning in your houses when you go to bed."

Sahih Al-Bukhari, hadith number 6293

قَالَ رَسُولُ اللهِ صَلَّى اللهُ عَلَيْهِ وَسَلَّمَ " مَا مِنْ أَحَدٍ يَدْعُو بِدُعَاءٍ إِلاَّ آتَاهُ اللهُ مَا سَأَلَ أَوْ كَفَّ عَنْهُ مِنَ السُّوءِ مِثْلَهُ مَا لَمْ يَدْعُ بِإِثْمٍ أَوْ قَطِيعَةِ رَحِمٍ ".

The Messenger of Allah(ﷺ) said, "There is no person who supplicates with a supplication except that Allah gives him what he asked, or averts from him an equivalent evil, as long as he does not supplicate for something sinful or for the severance of family ties."

Sahih Al Tirmidhi, hadith number 3381

قَالَ رَسُولُ اللهِ صَلَّى اللهُ عَلَيْهِ وَسَلَّمَ " لاَ تَتَمَنَّوْا لِقَاءَ الْعَدُوِّ، وَسَلُوا اللهَ الْعَافِيَةَ ".

The Messenger of Allah (ﷺ) said, "Do not wish to encounter the enemy, but ask Allah for well-being and safety."

Sahih Al-Bukhari, hadith number 7237

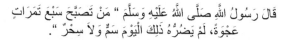

قَالَ رَسُولُ اللَّهِ صَلَّى اللَّهُ عَلَيْهِ وَسَلَّمَ " مَنْ تَصَبَّحَ سَبْعَ تَمَرَاتٍ عَجْوَةً، لَمْ يَضُرُّهُ ذَلِكَ الْيَوْمَ سَمٌّ وَلاَ سِحْرٌ ".

The Messenger of Allah (ﷺ) said, "Whoever eats seven 'Ajwa dates in the morning, will not be harmed by anything that day, neither poison nor sorcery."

Sahih Al-Bukhari, hadith number 5769

قَالَ رَسُولُ اللَّهِ صَلَّى اللَّهُ عَلَيْهِ وَسَلَّمَ " مَنْ أَصْبَحَ مِنْكُمْ مُعَافًى فِي جَسَدِهِ آمِنًا فِي سِرْبِهِ عِنْدَهُ قُوتُ يَوْمِهِ فَكَأَنَّمَا حِيزَتْ لَهُ الدُّنْيَا " .

The Messenger of Allah (ﷺ) said, "Whoever among you wakes up physically healthy, feels secure within himself and has food for the day, it is as if he has acquired the whole world."

Sunan Ibn Mayah, hadith number 4141

قَالَ رَسُولُ اللَّهِ صَلَّى اللَّهُ عَلَيْهِ وَسَلَّمَ " لَنْ يُوَافِيَ عَبْدٌ يَوْمَ الْقِيَامَةِ يَقُولُ لاَ إِلَهَ إِلاَّ اللَّهُ. يَبْتَغِي بِهِ وَجْهَ اللَّهِ، إِلاَّ حَرَّمَ اللَّهُ عَلَيْهِ النَّارَ ".

The Messenger of Allah (ﷺ) said, "If anybody comes on the Day of Resurrection who has said "La ilaha illal-lah" and intends to earn Allah's favor, He will forbid him the Hellfire."

Sahih Al-Bukhari, hadith number 6423

HADITHS ON SAFETY AND SECURITY

قَالَ رَسُولُ اللهِ صَلَّى اللهُ عَلَيْهِ وَسَلَّمَ " [...] اتَّقُوا النَّارَ وَلَوْ بِشِقِّ تَمْرَةٍ، فَمَنْ لَمْ يَجِدْ فَبِكَلِمَةٍ طَيِّبَةٍ " .

The Messenger of Allah (ﷺ) said, "[...] Protect yourselves
from the Fire, even if it is with half a date (as a gift),
and whoever does not even have that let him protect
himself by saying a good and pleasant word."

Sahih Al-Bukhari, Hadith number 6540

قَالَ رَسُولُ اللهِ صَلَّى اللهُ عَلَيْهِ وَسَلَّمَ " مَنْ سُئِلَ عَنْ عِلْمٍ
يَعْلَمُهُ فَكَتَمَهُ أُلْجِمَ يَوْمَ الْقِيَامَةِ بِلِجَامٍ مِنْ نَارٍ " .

The Messenger of Allah said, "Whoever is asked about
his knowledge and conceals it, will be punished
with reins of fire on the Day of Resurrection.'"

Sunan Ibn Mayah, hadith number 266

قَالَ رَسُولُ اللهِ صَلَّى اللهُ عَلَيْهِ وَسَلَّمَ: " أَلَا أُخْبِرُكُم بِمَنْ يَحْرُمُ عَلَى النَّارِ ،
أَوْ بِمِنْ تَحْرُمُ عَلَيْهِ النَّارُ ؟ تَحْرُمُ عَلَى كُلِّ قَرِيبٍ هَيِّنٍ لِينٍ سَهْلٍ " .

The Messenger of Allah (ﷺ) said, "Shall I tell you whom the Fire
of Hell may not touch? It is forbidden to touch a person who is
always approachable and has a courteous and tender character."

Riyad as-Salihin, hadith number 641

HADITHS ON SAFETY AND SECURITY

أَتَيْتُ النَّبِيَّ صَلَّى اللهُ عَلَيْهِ وَسَلَّمَ فَقُلْتُ عَلَيْكَ السَّلاَمُ يَا رَسُولَ اللهِ . قَالَ
" لاَ تَقُلْ عَلَيْكَ السَّلاَمُ فَإِنَّ عَلَيْكَ السَّلاَمُ تَحِيَّةُ الْمَوْتَى " .

I approached the Prophet (ﷺ) and said, "Upon you be peace, Messenger of Allah!" He replied, "Do not say, 'Peace be upon you, for that is the greeting to the dead. '

Sunan Abu Dawûd, hadith number 5209

[...] سَمِعْتُ رَسُولَ اللهِ صَلَّى اللهُ عَلَيْهِ وَسَلَّمَ يَقُولُ " مَا مِنْ شَيْءٍ يُصِيبُ الْمُؤْمِنَ
حَتَّى الشَّوْكَةِ تُصِيبُهُ إِلاَّ كَتَبَ اللهُ لَهُ بِهَا حَسَنَةً أَوْ حُطَّتْ عَنْهُ بِهَا خَطِيئَةً " .

I heard the Messenger of Allah (ﷺ) say, "There is nothing that befalls a believer, even if it is only the prick of a thorn, that Allah does not consider good for him or erase his sins."

Sahih Muslim, hadith number 2572 g

قَالَ النَّبِيُّ صَلَّى اللهُ عَلَيْهِ وَسَلَّمَ " قَالَ لِي جِبْرِيلُ مَنْ مَاتَ مِنْ أُمَّتِكَ لاَ يُشْرِكُ بِاللهِ
شَيْئًا دَخَلَ الْجَنَّةَ، أَوْ لَمْ يَدْخُلِ النَّارَ، قَالَ وَإِنْ زَنَى وَإِنْ سَرَقَ قَالَ وَإِنْ " .

The Prophet (ﷺ) said, "Jibril (Gabriel) said to me, 'Whoever of your followers dies without worshipping other than Allah will enter Paradise (or will not enter the Fire (of Hell).' The Prophet (ﷺ) asked. "Even if he has committed theft or adultery?' He said, 'Even if he committed theft or adultery.'"

Sahih Al-Bukhari, hadith number 3222

HADITHS ON SAFETY AND SECURITY

قَالَ النَّبِيُّ صَلَّى اللهُ عَلَيْهِ وَسَلَّمَ " إِنَّ الْعَبْدَ لَيَتَكَلَّمُ بِالْكَلِمَةِ مِنْ رِضْوَانِ اللهِ لاَ يُلْقِي لَهَا بَالاً، يَرْفَعُ اللهُ بِهَا دَرَجَاتٍ، وَإِنَّ الْعَبْدَ لَيَتَكَلَّمُ بِالْكَلِمَةِ مِنْ سَخَطِ اللهِ لاَ يُلْقِي لَهَا بَالاً يَهْوِي بِهَا فِي جَهَنَّمَ " .

The Prophet (ﷺ) said, "A muslim may utter a word that pleases Allah without attaching much importance to it, and thereby Allah will raise him to higher ranks. A muslim may utter a word that displeases Allah without thinking of its weight, and thereby he will be cast into the Hellfire."

Sahih Al-Bukhari, hadith number 6478

قَالَ النَّبِيُّ صَلَّى اللهُ عَلَيْهِ وَسَلَّمَ " مَنْ صَلَّى الصُّبْحَ فَهُوَ فِي ذِمَّةِ اللهِ عَزَّ وَجَلَّ " .

The Prophet (ﷺ) said, "Whoever performs the morning prayer is under the protection of Allah, Mighty and Exalted be He."

Sunan Ibn Mayah, hadith number 3946

HADITHS ON INTERPERSONAL BEHAVIOR

قَالَ رَسُولُ اللهِ صَلَّى اللهُ عَلَيْهِ وَسَلَّمَ " لاَ تُظْهِرِ الشَّمَاتَةَ لأَخِيكَ فَيَرْحَمُهُ اللهُ وَيَبْتَلِيكَ " .

The Messenger of Allah (ﷺ) said, "Do not rejoice in the misfortunes of your brother, that Allah may have mercy on him and put you to the test."

Sunan Al Tirmidhi, hadith number 2506

قَالَ رَسُولُ اللهِ صَلَّى اللهُ عَلَيْهِ وَسَلَّمَ " إِنِّي خَرَجْتُ لأُخْبِرَكُمْ بِلَيْلَةِ الْقَدْرِ، وَإِنَّهُ تَلاَحَى فُلاَنٌ وَفُلاَنٌ فَرُفِعَتْ وَعَسَى أَنْ يَكُونَ خَيْرًا لَكُمْ ".

The Prophet (ﷺ) said, "I went out to inform you about the date of the night of Al-Qadr, but as such and such argued, my knowledge was taken away (I forgot) and perhaps it is better for you."

Sahih Al-Bukhari, hadith number 49

عَنْ قَتَادَةَ، قَالَ " قُلْتُ لأَنَسٍ أَكَانَتِ الْمُصَافَحَةُ فِي أَصْحَابِ النَّبِيِّ صَلَّى اللهُ عَلَيْهِ وَسَلَّمَ قَالَ نَعَمْ ".

Qatada said, I asked Anas, "Was it customary for the companions of the Prophet (ﷺ) to shake hands with one another?" He said yes.

Sahih Al-Bukhari, hadith number 6263

HADITHS ON INTERPERSONAL BEHAVIOR

قَالَ النَّبِيُّ صَلَّى اللهُ عَلَيْهِ وَسَلَّمَ " لَا يُؤْمِنُ أَحَدُكُمْ حَتَّى يُحِبَّ لِأَخِيهِ مَا يُحِبُّ لِنَفْسِهِ ".

The Prophet (ﷺ) said, "None of you truly believes until he loves for his brother what he loves for himself."

Sahih Al-Bukhari, hadith number 13

نَهَى النَّبِيُّ صَلَّى اللهُ عَلَيْهِ وَسَلَّمَ أَنْ يَقْرُنَ الرَّجُلُ بَيْنَ التَّمْرَتَيْنِ جَمِيعًا، حَتَّى يَسْتَأْذِنَ أَصْحَابَهُ (الذين يشاركهم الطعام).

The Prophet (ﷺ) decreed that you should not eat two dates at the same time unless you get permission from your companions (who share the food with you).

Sahih Al-Bukhari, hadith number 2489

[...] إِنَّ لِي عَشَرَةً مِنَ الْوَلَدِ مَا قَبَّلْتُ مِنْهُمْ أَحَدًا. فَنَظَرَ إِلَيْهِ رَسُولُ اللهِ صَلَّى اللهُ عَلَيْهِ وَسَلَّمَ ثُمَّ قَالَ " مَنْ لَا يَرْحَمْ لَا يُرْحَمْ ".

"I have ten children and I have never kissed any of them." The Messenger of Allah (ﷺ) glanced at him and said, "Whoever is not merciful to others will not be treated with mercy."

Sahih Al-Bukhari, hadith number 5997

HADITHS ON INTERPERSONAL BEHAVIOR

قَالَ النَّبِيُّ صَلَّى اللهُ عَلَيْهِ وَسَلَّمَ " الْمُسْلِمَ إِذَا كَانَ يُخَالِطُ النَّاسَ وَيَصْبِرُ عَلَى أَذَاهُمْ خَيْرٌ مِنَ الْمُسْلِمِ الَّذِي لاَ يُخَالِطُ النَّاسَ وَلاَ يَصْبِرُ عَلَى أَذَاهُمْ " .

The Prophet (ﷺ) said, "A Muslim who mingles with the people and endures their harm is better than the Muslim who does not mingle with the people and does not endure their harm."

Sunan Al Tirmidhi, hadith number 2507

قَالَ النَّبِيُّ صَلَّى اللهُ عَلَيْهِ وَسَلَّمَ " إِذَا قَاتَلَ أَحَدُكُمْ أَخَاهُ فَلْيَجْتَنِبِ الْوَجْهَ فَإِنَّ اللَّهَ خَلَقَ آدَمَ عَلَى صُورَتِهِ " .

The Prophet (ﷺ) said, "When one of you fights his brother, let him avoid striking the face, for indeed, Allah created Adam in His image."

Sahih Muslim, hadith number 2612 e

قَالَ رَسُولُ اللَّهِ صَلَّى اللهُ عَلَيْهِ وَسَلَّمَ " مَا مِنْ جَرْعَةٍ أَعْظَمَ عِنْدَ اللهِ أَجْرًا مِنْ جَرْعَةِ غَيْظٍ كَظَمَهَا عَبْدٌ ابْتِغَاءَ وَجْهِ اللهِ " .

The Messenger of Allah (ﷺ) said, "There is nothing more rewarded by Allah than a servant of Allah who restrains his anger for the sake of Allah."

Al Adab Al Mufrad, hadith number 1318

HADITHS ON INTERPERSONAL BEHAVIOR

قَالَ رَسُولُ اللَّهِ صَلَّى اللَّهُ عَلَيْهِ وَسَلَّمَ " الرَّجُلُ عَلَى دِينِ خَلِيلِهِ فَلْيَنْظُرْ أَحَدُكُمْ مَنْ يُخَالِلُ " .

The Prophet (ﷺ) said, "A person follows the religion of his friend; so everyone should consider whom he makes friends with."

Sunan Abu Dawûd, hadith number 4833

قَالَ رَسُولُ اللَّهِ صَلَّى اللَّهُ عَلَيْهِ وَسَلَّمَ " لاَ يُقِيمُ الرَّجُلُ الرَّجُلَ مِنْ مَجْلِسِهِ، ثُمَّ يَجْلِسُ فِيهِ " .

The Prophet (ﷺ) said, "A man should not make another man get up from his seat (in a gathering) to sit in his place."

Sahih Al-Bukhari, Hadith number 6269

قَالَ رَسُولُ اللَّهِ صَلَّى اللَّهُ عَلَيْهِ وَسَلَّمَ: "يَسِّرَا وَلاَ تُعَسِّرَا، وَبَشِّرَا وَلاَ تُنَفِّرَا، وَتَطَاوَعَا وَلاَ تَخْتَلِفَا " .

The Prophet (ﷺ) said, "Make things easy and do not make them difficult, give glad tidings and do not create aversion, cooperate with each other and do not break off relations."

Sahih Al-Bukhari, hadith number 3038

HADITHS ON INTERPERSONAL BEHAVIOR

قَالَ رَسُولُ اللهِ صَلَّى اللهُ عَلَيْهِ وَسَلَّمَ: " طَلَبُ الْعِلْمِ فَرِيضَةٌ عَلَى كُلِّ مُسْلِمٍ وَوَاضِعُ الْعِلْمِ عِنْدَ غَيْرِ أَهْلِهِ كَمُقَلِّدِ الْخَنَازِيرِ الْجَوْهَرَ وَاللُّؤْلُؤَ وَالذَّهَبَ " .

The Messenger of Allah (ﷺ) said, "The pursuit of knowledge is a duty for every Muslim, and whoever conveys knowledge to those who do not deserve it is like one who puts a necklace of jewels, pearls and gold on the necks of pigs."

Sunan Ibn Mayah, hadith number 224

قَالَ رَسُولُ اللهِ صَلَّى اللهُ عَلَيْهِ وَسَلَّمَ: " لا يَسْتُرُ عَبْدٌ عَبْدًا فِي الدُّنيا إلا سَتَرَه اللهُ يومَ القِيامةِ " .

The Prophet (ﷺ) said, "No servant conceals (the faults) of another servant in this world except that Allah will conceal his faults on the Day of Resurrection."

Riyad as-Salihin, hadith number 240

قَالَ رَسُولُ اللهِ صَلَّى اللهُ عَلَيْهِ وَسَلَّمَ: " لاَ يَشْكُرُ اللهَ مَنْ لاَ يَشْكُرُ النَّاسَ " .

The Prophet (ﷺ) said, "Whoever does not thank people is not grateful to Allah."

Sunan Abu Dawûd, hadith number 4811

HADITHS ON INTERPERSONAL BEHAVIOR

قَالَ رَسُولُ اللهِ صَلَّى اللهُ عَلَيْهِ وَسَلَّمَ: " لَيْسَ الْكَذَّابُ الَّذِي يُصْلِحُ بَيْنَ النَّاسِ، فَيَنْمِي خَيْرًا، أَوْ يَقُولُ خَيْرًا ".

The Messenger of Allah (ﷺ) said, "Whoever makes peace between people by inventing good information or saying good things is not a liar."

Sahih Al-Bukhari, hadith number 2692

سَأَلَ رجلٌ رسولَ اللهِ صَلَّى اللهُ عَلَيْهِ وَسَلَّمَ: أي الإسلام خير؟ قَالَ: "تُطعِمُ الطعامَ، وتَقرأ السَّلامَ عَلَى مَنْ عَرِفتَ ومَنْ لم تَعرِف".

A man asked the Messenger of Allah (ﷺ), "What is the best action in Islam?" He replied, "To feed and greet everyone, whether you know them or not."

Riyad as-Salihin, hadith number 844

قَالَ رَسُولُ اللهِ صَلَّى اللهُ عَلَيْهِ وَسَلَّمَ " لَيْسَ الْمُؤْمِنُ بِالطَّعَّانِ وَلاَ اللَّعَّانِ وَلاَ الْفَاحِشِ وَلاَ الْبَذِيءِ " .

The Messenger of Allah (ﷺ) said, "The believer is not one who indulges in slandering, cursing, indecency, or vulgar speech."

Yam'a Al Tirmidhi, hadith number 1977

HADITHS ON INTERPERSONAL BEHAVIOR

قَالَ لِيَ النَّبِيُّ صَلَّى اللهُ عَلَيْهِ وَسَلَّمَ " لَا تَحْقِرَنَّ مِنَ الْمَعْرُوفِ شَيْئًا وَلَوْ أَنْ تَلْقَى أَخَاكَ بِوَجْهٍ طَلْقٍ " .

The Messenger of Allah (ﷺ) said to me, "Do not belittle any act of kindness, even if it is meeting your brother with a cheerful face."

Sahih Muslim, hadith number 2626

قَالَ رَسُولُ اللهِ صَلَّى اللهُ عَلَيْهِ وَسَلَّمَ: " كل المسلم على المسلم حَرام: دَمهُ وعِرضهُ ومَالهُ ".

The Messenger of Allah (ﷺ) said, "Every Muslim's life, honor, and property are sacred and inviolable for another Muslim."

Riyad as-Salihin, hadith number 1527

قَالَ النَّبِيُّ صَلَّى اللهُ عَلَيْهِ وَسَلَّمَ: " أَدِّ الأَمَانَةَ إِلَى مَنِ انْتَمَنَكَ وَلاَ تَخُنْ مَنْ خَانَكَ " .

The Prophet (ﷺ) said, "Give back the trust to the one who entrusted you and do not betray the one who betrayed you."

Yam'a Al Tirmidhi, hadith number 1264

HADITHS ON INTERPERSONAL BEHAVIOR

قَالَ النَّبِيُّ صَلَّى اللهُ عَلَيْهِ وَسَلَّمَ " يَسِّرُوا وَلاَ تُعَسِّرُوا، وَسَكِّنُوا وَلاَ تُنَفِّرُوا ".

The Prophet (ﷺ) said, "Facilitate things for the people (treat them with ease and not difficulty) and do not make things difficult for them; give them good tidings and do not make them run away (from Islam)."

Sahih Al-Bukhari, hadith number 6125

قَالَ النَّبِيُّ صَلَّى اللَّهُ عَلَيْهِ وَسَلَّمَ: " لَيْسَ الْمُؤْمِنُ الَّذِي يَشْبَعُ وَجَارُهُ جَائِعٌ ".

The Prophet (ﷺ) said, "He is not a believer whose stomach is full while his neighbor is hungry."

Al Adab al Mufrad, hadith number 112

قَالَ رَسُولُ اللَّهِ صَلَّى اللَّهُ عَلَيْهِ وَسَلَّمَ: " لَيْسَ مِنَّا مَنْ لَمْ يَرْحَمْ صَغِيرَنَا وَيُوَقِّرْ كَبِيرَنَا."

The Messenger of Allah (ﷺ) said, "He is not one of us who does not show mercy to our young ones and respect to our elders."

Sahih Al Tirmidhi, hadith number 1920

قَالَ رَسُولُ اللَّهِ صَلَّى اللَّهُ عَلَيْهِ وَسَلَّمَ: " طَعَامُ الِاثْنَيْنِ كَافِي الثَّلَاثَةِ وَطَعَامُ الثَّلَاثَةِ كَافِي الْأَرْبَعَةِ ".

The Messenger of Allah (ﷺ) said, "Food for two is enough for three people and food for three is enough for four people."

Sahih Muslim, hadith number 2058

HADITHS ON INTERPERSONAL BEHAVIOR

عَنْ مُجَاهِدٍ، عَنْ عَبْدِ اللَّهِ بْنِ عَمْرٍو، أَنَّهُ ذَبَحَ شَاةً فَقَالَ أَهْدَيْتُمْ لِجَارِي الْيَهُودِيِّ فَإِنِّي سَمِعْتُ رَسُولَ اللَّهِ صَلَّى اللَّهُ عَلَيْهِ وَسَلَّمَ يَقُولُ " مَا زَالَ جِبْرِيلُ يُوصِينِي بِالْجَارِ حَتَّى ظَنَنْتُ أَنَّهُ سَيُوَرِّثُهُ " .

Mujahid related that 'Abdullah ibn Amr slaughtered a sheep and asked, "Have you given a gift from it to our Jewish neighbor? For I heard the Messenger of Allah (ﷺ) saying, 'Jibril kept recommending treating neighbors with kindness until I thought he would assign them a share of inheritance.

Sunan Abu Dawûd, hadith number 5152

قَالَ رَسُولُ اللَّهِ صَلَّى اللَّهُ عَلَيْهِ وَسَلَّمَ " الْمُسْتَبَّانِ مَا قَالاَ فَعَلَى الْبَادِي مِنْهُمَا مَا لَمْ يَعْتَدِ الْمَظْلُومُ " .

The Messenger of Allah (ﷺ) said, "If two people insult each other, the person who started it is blamed for what they say, as long as the aggrieved person does not overstep the mark."

Sunan Abu Dawûd, hadith number 4894

عَنْ أَبِي خِرَاشٍ السُّلَمِيِّ، أَنَّهُ سَمِعَ رَسُولَ اللَّهِ صَلَّى اللَّهُ عَلَيْهِ وَسَلَّمَ يَقُولُ " مَنْ هَجَرَ أَخَاهُ سَنَةً فَهُوَ كَسَفْكِ دَمِهِ " .

Abu Jirash heard the Messenger of Allah (ﷺ) say, "If you cut relationships with your brother for a year, it is like shedding his blood."

Sunan Abu Dawûd, Hadith number 4915

HADITHS ON INTERPERSONAL BEHAVIOR

قَالَ رَسُولُ اللهِ صَلَّى اللهُ عَلَيْهِ وَسَلَّمَ " لاَ يَحِلُّ لِمُسْلِمٍ أَنْ يُرَوِّعَ مُسْلِمًا ".

The Prophet (ﷺ) said, "It is not lawful for a
Muslim to frighten another Muslim."

Sunan Abu Dawûd, hadith number 5004

قَالَ رَسُولُ اللهِ صَلَّى اللهُ عَلَيْهِ وَسَلَّمَ " خَمْسٌ تَجِبُ لِلْمُسْلِمِ عَلَى أَخِيهِ رَدُّ السَّلاَمِ
وَتَشْمِيتُ الْعَاطِسِ وَإِجَابَةُ الدَّعْوَةِ وَعِيَادَةُ الْمَرِيضِ وَاتِّبَاعُ الْجَنَازَةِ " .

The Messenger of Allah (ﷺ) said, "There are five qualities
that a Muslim should show towards his brother: returning
the greeting, responding to the one who sneezes, accepting
the invitation, visiting the sick, and attending the funeral."

Sunan Abu Dawûd, hadith number 5030

قَالَ رَسُولُ اللهِ صَلَّى اللهُ عَلَيْهِ وَسَلَّمَ: " لَأَنْ يَحْتَطِبَ أَحَدُكُمْ حُزْمَةً
عَلَى ظَهْرِهِ، خَيْرٌ لَهُ مِنْ أَنْ يَسْأَلَ أَحَدًا فَيُعْطِيَهُ أَوْ يَمْنَعَهُ ".

The Messenger of Allah (ﷺ) said, "It is better for someone
to carry a bundle of firewood on his back and sell it than
to beg of someone whether he gives him or refuses."

Riyad as-Salihin, hadith number 539

HADITHS ON INTERPERSONAL BEHAVIOR

قَالَ رَسُولُ اللهِ صَلَّى اللهُ عَلَيْهِ وَسَلَّمَ: " حَدِّثُوا عَنْ بَنِي إِسْرَائِيلَ وَلاَ حَرَجَ " .

The Prophet (ﷺ) said, "Narrate from the Children of Israel, and there is no harm in that."

Sunan Abu Dawûd, hadith number 3662

قَالَ رَسُولُ اللهِ صَلَّى اللهُ عَلَيْهِ وَسَلَّمَ: " مَنْ عُرِضَ عَلَيْهِ طِيبٌ فَلاَ يَرُدَّهُ فَإِنَّهُ طَيِّبُ الرِّيحِ خَفِيفُ الْمَحْمَلِ " .

The Messenger of Allah (ﷺ) said, "If someone is given perfume, he should not return it; for it is something of good smell and easy to wear."

Sunan Abu Dawûd, hadith number 4172

عَنِ ابْنِ مَسْعُودٍ، قَالَ " كَانَ النَّبِيُّ صَلَّى اللهُ عَلَيْهِ وَسَلَّمَ يَتَخَوَّلُنَا بِالْمَوْعِظَةِ فِي الأَيَّامِ، كَرَاهَةَ السَّآمَةِ عَلَيْنَا " .

Ibn Mas'ud related, "The Prophet (ﷺ) always took care of us while preaching by choosing a suitable time so that we would not be bored. (He refrained from bothering us with sermons and knowledge all the time)."

Sahih Al-Bukhari, hadith number 68

HADITHS ON BEHAVIOR TOWARDS ANIMALS AND THE ENVIRONMENT

سَأَلَ الصَّحَابَةِ النَّبِيِّ ﷺ، و قَالوا: يا رسولَ اللهِ و إنَّ لنا في
البهائمِ أجرًا ؟ قال: " في كُلِّ كَبِدٍ رطْبَةٍ أجرٌ ".

The Companions asked the Prophet (ﷺ), "Shall we also be
rewarded for being kind to animals? The Prophet (ﷺ) replied,
"A reward is given in relation to every living creature."

Riyad as-Salihin, hadith number 126

قَالَ رَسُولُ اللهِ صَلَّى اللهُ عَلَيْهِ وَسَلَّمَ: " خَلَقَ اللهُ مِائَةَ رَحْمَةٍ فَوَضَعَ رَحْمَةً
وَاحِدَةً بَيْنَ خَلْقِهِ يَتَرَاحَمُونَ بِهَا وَ عِنْدَ اللهِ تِسْعَةً وَتِسْعُونَ رَحْمَةً ".

The Messenger of Allah (ﷺ) said, "Allah has created one
hundred mercies and has placed one of them in His
creation so that the creatures may be merciful to one
another. And there are ninety-nine mercies with Allah."

Sahih Al Tirmidhi, hadith number 3541

قَالَ رَسُولُ اللهِ صَلَّى اللهُ عَلَيْهِ وَسَلَّمَ " عُذِّبَتِ امْرَأَةٌ في هِرَّةٍ أَوْثَقَتْهَا فَلَمْ
تُطْعِمْهَا وَلَمْ تَسْقِهَا وَلَمْ تَدَعْهَا تَأْكُلُ مِنْ خَشَاشِ الأَرْضِ ".

The Messenger of Allah (ﷺ) said, "A woman was punished
because of a cat (in Hell). She tied it up and gave it neither food
nor drink and did not release it to eat the vermin of the earth."

Sahih Muslim, hadith number 2242 d

HADITHS ON BEHAVIOR TOWARDS ANIMALS AND THE ENVIRONMENT

قَالَ رَسُولُ اللهِ صَلَّى اللهُ عَلَيْهِ وَسَلَّمَ " غُفِرَ لِامْرَأَةٍ مُومِسَةٍ مَرَّتْ بِكَلْبٍ عَلَى رَأْسِ رَكِيٍّ يَلْهَثُ، قَالَ كَادَ يَقْتُلُهُ الْعَطَشُ، فَنَزَعَتْ خُفَّهَا، فَأَوْثَقَتْهُ بِخِمَارِهَا، فَنَزَعَتْ لَهُ مِنَ الْمَاءِ، فَغُفِرَ لَهَا بِذَلِكَ " .

The Messenger of Allah (ﷺ) said, "A prostitute was forgiven by Allah because when she passed by a panting dog near a well and saw that the dog was about to die of thirst, she took off her shoe and tied it on her head to bring water to the dog. For that Allah forgave her."

Sahih Al-Bukhari, hadith number 3321

قَالَ رَسُولُ اللهِ صَلَّى اللهُ عَلَيْهِ وَسَلَّمَ " مَنِ اتَّخَذَ كَلْبًا إِلاَّ كَلْبَ مَاشِيَةٍ أَوْ صَيْدٍ أَوْ زَرْعٍ انْتَقَصَ مِنْ أَجْرِهِ كُلَّ يَوْمٍ قِيرَاطٌ " .

The Prophet (ﷺ) said, "Whoever has a dog, except a sheepdog, a hunting dog or a farm dog, will have something deducted from his reward every day."

Sunan Abu Dawûd, hadith number 2844

مَرَّ رَسُولُ اللهِ صَلَّى اللهُ عَلَيْهِ وَسَلَّمَ بِبَعِيرٍ قَدْ لَحِقَ ظَهْرُهُ بِبَطْنِهِ، فَقَالَ: " اتَّقُوا اللهَ فِي هَذِهِ الْبَهَائِمِ الْمُعْجَمَةِ فَارْكَبُوهَا وَكُلُوهَا صَالِحَةً " .

The Messenger of Allah (ﷺ) passed by a camel whose back had almost reached its belly due to extreme thinness. He said, "Fear Allah regarding these mute animals that cannot speak. Ride them when they are in good condition and feed them when they are healthy."

Sunan Abu Dawûd, Hadith number 2548

HADITHS ON BEHAVIOR TOWARDS ANIMALS AND THE ENVIRONMENT

قَالَ رَسُولُ اللهِ صَلَّى اللهُ عَلَيْهِ وَسَلَّمَ " ارْتَبِطُوا الْخَيْلَ وَامْسَحُوا بِنَوَاصِيهَا وَأَعْجَازِهَا " . أَوْ قَالَ " أَكْفَالِهَا " . " وَقَلِّدُوهَا وَلاَ تُقَلِّدُوهَا الأَوْتَارَ " .

The Messenger of Allah (ﷺ) said, "Tie up the horses, rub their forelegs and buttocks, and put things around their necks, but do not shackle them."

Sunan Abu Dawúd, hadith number 2553

قَالَ رَسُولُ اللهِ صَلَّى اللهُ عَلَيْهِ وَسَلَّمَ " بَيْنَمَا رَجُلٌ يَمْشِي بِطَرِيقٍ اشْتَدَّ عَلَيْهِ الْعَطَشُ، فَوَجَدَ بِئْراً فَنَزَلَ فِيهَا فَشَرِبَ، ثُمَّ خَرَجَ فَإِذَا كَلْبٌ يَلْهَثُ يَأْكُلُ الثَّرَى مِنَ الْعَطَشِ، فَقَالَ الرَّجُلُ: لَقَدْ بَلَغَ هَذَا الْكَلْبَ مِنَ العطشِ مِثْلَ الَّذِي كَانَ قَدْ بَلَغَ مِنِّي، فَنَزَلَ الْبِئْرَ فَمَلأَ خُفَّهُ مَاءً ثُمَّ أَمْسَكَهُ بِفِيهِ، حتَّى رقِيَ فَسَقَى الْكَلْبَ، فَشَكَرَ اللَّهُ لَه فَغَفَرَ لَهُ. قَالُوا: يَا رسولَ اللهِ إِنَّ لَنَا فِي الْبَهَائِمِ أَجْراً؟ فَقَالَ: "فِي كُلِّ كَبِدٍ رَطْبَةٍ أَجْرٌ ".

The Prophet (ﷺ) said, "A man felt very thirsty while traveling, so he came to a well. He went down to the well, quenched his thirst and came out again. In the meantime, he saw a dog panting and licking mud because he was so thirsty. He said to himself, "This dog is as thirsty as I am." So he went back down to the well, filled his shoe with water and soaked it. Allah thanked him for this action and forgave him. The people said, "O Messenger of Allah (ﷺ), is there any reward for us if we serve animals?" He replied, "Yes, there is reward for serving every living creature."

Sahih Al-Bukhari, hadith number 2466

HADITHS ON BEHAVIOR TOWARDS ANIMALS AND THE ENVIRONMENT

عَنْ عُتْبَةَ بْنِ عَبْدٍ السُّلَمِيِّ، أَنَّهُ سَمِعَ رَسُولَ اللهِ صَلَّى اللهُ عَلَيْهِ وَسَلَّمَ يَقُولُ: " لاَ تَقُصُّوا نَوَاصِيَ الْخَيْلِ وَلاَ مَعَارِفَهَا وَلاَ أَذْنَابَهَا، فَإِنَّ أَذْنَابَهَا مَذَابُّهَا، وَمَعَارِفَهَا دِفَاؤُهَا، وَنَوَاصِيهَا مَعْقُودٌ فِيهَا الْخَيْرُ ".

Utba heard the Messenger of Allah (ﷺ) say, "Do not cut the topknot, mane or tail of horses, for with the tail they drive away the flies, the mane warms them and the topknot is blessed."

Sunan Abu Dawûd, hadith number 2542

قَالَ رَسُولُ اللهِ صَلَّى اللهُ عَلَيْهِ وَسَلَّمَ " الْهِرَّةُ لاَ تَقْطَعُ الصَّلاَةَ لأَنَّهَا مِنْ مَتَاعِ الْبَيْتِ ".

The Messenger of Allah (ﷺ) said, "Cats do not invalidate prayer, for they are among the useful things in the house."

Sunan Ibn Mayah, hadith number 369

قَالَ رَسُولُ اللهِ صَلَّى اللهُ عَلَيْهِ وَسَلَّمَ: " مَا مِنْ مُسْلِمٍ يَغْرِسُ غَرْسًا أَوْ يَزْرَعُ زَرْعًا فَيَأْكُلُ مِنْهُ إِنْسَانٌ أَوْ طَيْرٌ أَوْ بَهِيمَةٌ إِلاَّ كَانَتْ لَهُ صَدَقَةٌ ".

The Messenger of Allah (ﷺ) said, "If a Muslim plants a crop or sows a crop from which a person, bird or animal then eats, it will be counted as charity."

Sahih Al Tirmidhi, hadith number 1382

HADITHS ON BEHAVIOR TOWARDS ANIMALS AND THE ENVIRONMENT

عَنْ دَاوُدَ بْنِ صَالِحِ بْنِ دِينَارٍ التَّمَّارِ ، عَنْ أُمِّهِ ، أَنَّ مَوْلاَتَهَا ، أَرْسَلَتْهَا بِهَرِيسَةٍ إِلَى عَائِشَةَ رضى الله عنها فَوَجَدْتُهَا تُصَلِّي فَأَشَارَتْ إِلَيَّ أَنْ ضَعِيهَا فَجَاءَتْ هِرَّةٌ فَأَكَلَتْ مِنْهَا فَلَمَّا انْصَرَفَتْ أَكَلَتْ مِنْ حَيْثُ أَكَلَتِ الْهِرَّةُ فَقَالَتْ إِنَّ رَسُولَ اللَّهِ صلى الله عليه وسلم قَالَ " إِنَّهَا لَيْسَتْ بِنَجَسٍ إِنَّمَا هِيَ مِنَ الطَّوَّافِينَ عَلَيْكُمْ " . وَقَدْ رَأَيْتُ رَسُولَ اللَّهِ صلى الله عليه وسلم يَتَوَضَّأُ بِفَضْلِهَا .

Dawud ibn Salih ibn Dinar Al Tammar quoted his mother as saying that her mistress sent her with some pudding (harisah) to Aisha, who was performing the prayer. She instructed me to leave it on the floor. A cat came and ate some of it, but when Aisha finished her prayer, she ate from the place where the cat had eaten. The Messenger of Allah (ﷺ) said, "She is not impure; she is of those who roam among you." He added, "I saw the Messenger of Allah (ﷺ) making ablutions with the water left by the cat."

Sunan Abu Dawûd, hadith number 76

سَمِعْتُ الشَّرِيدَ ، يَقُولُ سَمِعْتُ رَسُولَ اللَّهِ صَلَّى اللَّهُ عَلَيْهِ وَسَلَّمَ يَقُولُ " مَنْ قَتَلَ عُصْفُورًا عَبَثًا عَجَّ إِلَى اللَّهِ عَزَّ وَجَلَّ يَوْمَ الْقِيَامَةِ يَقُولُ يَا رَبِّ إِنَّ فُلاَنًا قَتَلَنِي عَبَثًا وَلَمْ يَقْتُلْنِي لِمَنْفَعَةٍ " .

I heard Sharid say: 'I heard Allah's Messenger (ﷺ) say: "Whoever kills a little bird for no reason, that bird will supplicate to Allah on the Day of Resurrection and say, "O Lord, so-and-so killed me for no reason. And he did not kill me for a useful purpose'."

Sunan Al-Nasa'i, hadith number 4446

HADITHS ON BEHAVIOR TOWARDS ANIMALS AND THE ENVIRONMENT

[...] مَنْ فَعَلَ هَذَا؟ لَعَنَ اللهُ مَنْ فَعَلَ هَذَا. إِنَّ رَسُولَ اللهِ صَلَّى اللهُ عَلَيْهِ وَسَلَّمَ لَعَنَ مَنِ اتَّخَذَ شَيْئًا فِيهِ الرُّوحُ غَرَضًا .

[...] Who has done this? Allah has cursed the one who does this. Indeed, the Messenger of Allah (ﷺ) has cursed the one who makes a living creature a target of his shooting.

Sahih Muslim, hadith number 1958 b

عَنْ عَبْدِ اللهِ، أَنَّ النَّبِيَّ صَلَّى اللهُ عَلَيْهِ وَسَلَّمَ نَزَلَ مَنْزِلاً فَأَخَذَ رَجُلٌ بَيْضَ حُمَّرَةٍ، فَجَاءَتْ تَرِفُّ عَلَى رَأْسِ رَسُولِ اللهِ صَلَّى اللهُ عَلَيْهِ وَسَلَّمَ فَقَالَ: " أَيُّكُمْ فَجَعَ هَذِهِ بِبَيْضَتِهَا؟ فَقَالَ رَجُلٌ: يَا رَسُولَ اللهِ، أَنَا أَخَذْتُ بَيْضَتَهَا، فَقَالَ النَّبِيُّ صلى الله عليه وسلم: ارْدُدْ، رَحْمَةً لَهَا ".

'Abdullah related that the Prophet (ﷺ) stopped at a place and then someone took the eggs of a bird and it began to flap its wings around the head of the Messenger of Allah (ﷺ). He asked, "Which of you took her eggs?" A man said, "Messenger of Allah, I took the eggs." The Messenger of Allah (ﷺ) said, "Give them back to the bird out of mercy."

Al Adab al Mufrad, hadith number 382

HADITHS ON BEHAVIOR TOWARDS ANIMALS AND THE ENVIRONMENT

سَمِعْتُ رَسُولَ اللَّهِ صَلَّى اللَّهُ عَلَيْهِ وَسَلَّمَ يَقُولُ " قَرَصَتْ نَمْلَةٌ نَبِيًّا مِنَ الأَنْبِيَاءِ، فَأَمَرَ بِقَرْيَةِ النَّمْلِ فَأُحْرِقَتْ، فَأَوْحَى اللَّهُ إِلَيْهِ أَنْ قَرَصَتْكَ نَمْلَةٌ أَحْرَقْتَ أُمَّةً مِنَ الأُمَمِ تُسَبِّحُ اللَّهِ ".

I heard the Messenger of Allah (ﷺ) say: "An ant stung a prophet and he ordered to burn the anthill. Then Allah inspired him, "Because you were stung by one ant, you have burned a whole people of ants who praise and glorify Allah?".

Sahih Al-Bukhari, hadith number 3019

إِنَّ النَّبِيَّ صَلَّى اللَّهُ عَلَيْهِ وَسَلَّمَ نَهَى عَنْ قَتْلِ أَرْبَعٍ مِنَ الدَّوَابِّ النَّمْلَةِ وَالنَّحْلَةِ وَالْهُدْهُدِ وَالصُّرَدُ .

The Prophet (ﷺ) forbade the killing of four living creatures: ants, bees, hoopoes and shrikes.

Sunan Abu Dawûd, hadith number 5267

قَالَ رَسُولُ اللَّهِ صَلَّى اللَّهُ عَلَيْهِ وَسَلَّمَ: " كُنْ فِي الدُّنْيَا كَأَنَّكَ غَرِيبٌ، أَوْ عَابِرُ سَبِيلٍ ".

The Messenger of Allah (ﷺ) said, "Be in this world as if you were a stranger or a traveller."

Sahih Al-Bukhari, hadith number 6416

نَهَى رَسُولُ اللَّهِ صَلَّى اللَّهُ عَلَيْهِ وَسَلَّمَ أَنْ يُبَالَ فِي الْمَاءِ الرَّاكِدِ .

The Messenger of Allah (ﷺ) forbade urinating in stagnant water.

Sahih Muslim, hadith number 281

"Be ye therefore steadfast. Verily, the promise of Allah is true. And those who are not convinced should not cause you to waver."

(Ar-Rum 30:60)

Please pause.

Ibrahim Al-Abadi and Path of Islam are convinced that Muslims must always remain united and strong to spread Islam together. So if you like this book, feel free to recommend it to your family, friends and relatives. Even non-Muslims can learn about Islam and find the path to Allah with the help of this book.

If you like this book, please support us by leaving an honest review.

You can rate the book using the following link or QR code:

[Link: https://www.amazon.co.uk/review/create-review/?ie=UTF8&channel=glan-%20ce-detail&asin=3989290681]

Have you found any errors? Of course we are open to your criticism and welcome your suggestions so that we can further develop this work to the greater satisfaction of Allah ﷻ.

Feel free to email us at **info@islamway-books.com**

Shkran!

Ibrahim Al-Abadi & Islam Way

HADITHS ON FORGIVENESS

يَحْكِي رَسُولُ اللَّهِ ـ صَلَّى اللَّهُ عَلَيْهِ وَسَلَّمَ ـ نَبِيًّا مِنَ الْأَنْبِيَاءِ ضَرَبَهُ قَوْمُهُ وَهُوَ
يَمْسَحُ الدَّمَ عَنْ وَجْهِهِ وَيَقُولُ "رَبِّ اغْفِرْ لِقَوْمِي فَإِنَّهُمْ لاَ يَعْلَمُونَ" .

The Messenger of Allah (ﷺ) narrated about a prophet
from the previous prophets who was beaten by his people
while he was wiping the blood from his face, saying, "O
Lord, forgive my people, for indeed, they do not know."

Sunan Ibn Mayah, hadith number 4025

قَالَ رَسُولُ اللَّهِ صَلَّى اللَّهُ عَلَيْهِ وَسَلَّمَ " مَنْ قَالَ سُبْحَانَ اللَّهِ وَبِحَمْدِهِ. فِي
يَوْمٍ مِائَةَ مَرَّةٍ حُطَّتْ خَطَايَاهُ، وَإِنْ كَانَتْ مِثْلَ زَبَدِ الْبَحْرِ " .

The Messenger of Allah (ﷺ) said, "Whoever says, ‹Subhan
Allah wa bihamdihi› a hundred times a day, all his sins will be
forgiven, even if they are as great as the foam of the sea."

Sahih Al-Bukhari, hadith number 6405

قَالَ رَسُولُ اللَّهِ صَلَّى اللَّهُ عَلَيْهِ وَسَلَّمَ " إِنَّ الرَّجُلَ لَتُرْفَعُ دَرَجَتُهُ فِي
الْجَنَّةِ فَيَقُولُ أَنَّى هَذَا فَيُقَالُ بِاسْتِغْفَارِ وَلَدِكَ لَكَ " .

The Messenger of Allah (ﷺ) said, "A man's status is
elevated in Paradise and he will say, 'Where did this
come from?' And it will be said to him, 'From your
son who prays asking forgiveness for you.'"

Sunan Ibn Mayah, hadith number 3660

HADITHS ON FORGIVENESS

سَمِعْتُ رسولَ اللهِ صَلَّى اللهُ عَلَيْهِ وَسَلَّمَ يقول " وَاللهِ إِنِّي لأَسْتَغْفِرُ اللهَ وَأَتُوبُ إِلَيْهِ فِي الْيَوْمِ أَكْثَرَ مِنْ سَبْعِينَ مَرَّةً ".

I heard the Messenger of Allah (ﷺ) say, "I swear by Allah that I seek Allah's forgiveness and turn to Him in repentance more than seventy times a day."

Riyad as-Salihin, Hadith number 1870

قَالَ رَسُولُ اللهِ صَلَّى اللهُ عَلَيْهِ وَسَلَّمَ " وَالَّذِي نَفْسِي بِيَدِهِ لَوْ لَمْ تُذْنِبُوا لَذَهَبَ اللهُ تَعَالَى بِكُمْ، وَلَجَاءَ بِقَوْمٍ يُذْنِبُونَ فَيَسْتَغْفِرُونَ اللهَ تَعَالَى فَيَغْفِرُ لَهُمْ ".

The Messenger of Allah (ﷺ) said, "By the One in Whose hand is my soul, if you did not commit sins, Allah would substitute for you a people who commit sins and then ask Allah for forgiveness; and Allah would forgive them."

Riyad as-Salihin, hadith number 422

سَمِعْتُ رَسُولَ اللهِ صَلَّى اللهُ عَلَيْهِ وَسَلَّمَ يَقُولُ " وَاللهِ إِنِّي لأَسْتَغْفِرُ اللهَ وَأَتُوبُ إِلَيْهِ فِي الْيَوْمِ أَكْثَرَ مِنْ سَبْعِينَ مَرَّةً ".

I heard Allah's Messenger (ﷺ) say, "By Allah, I ask Allah for forgiveness and turn to Him in repentance more than seventy times a day."

Sahih Al-Bukhari, hadith number 6307

HADITHS ON FORGIVENESS

سَمِعْتُ رَسُولَ اللهِ صَلَّى اللهُ عَلَيْهِ وَسَلَّمَ يَقُولُ لِرَمَضَانَ " مَنْ قَامَهُ إِيمَانًا وَاحْتِسَابًا غُفِرَ لَهُ مَا تَقَدَّمَ مِنْ ذَنْبِهِ ".

I heard the Messenger of Allah (ﷺ) say about Ramadan, "Whoever prays in the month of Ramadan at night out of sincere faith and in the hope of a reward from Allah, all his previous sins will be forgiven him."

Sahih Al-Bukhari, hadith number 2008

قَالَ رَسُولُ اللهِ صَلَّى اللهُ عَلَيْهِ وَسَلَّمَ " حِينَ يَخْرُجُ الرَّجُلُ مِنْ بَيْتِهِ إِلَى مَسْجِدِهِ فَرِجْلٌ تُكْتَبُ حَسَنَةً وَرِجْلٌ تَمْحُو سَيِّئَةً ".

The Messenger of Allah (ﷺ) said, "When a man leaves his house for the mosque, one foot records a good deed and the other erases a bad deed."

Sunan Al-Nasa'i, hadith number 705

قَالَ رَسُولُ اللهِ صَلَّى اللهُ عَلَيْهِ وَسَلَّمَ: " مَنْ تَوَضَّأَ فَأَحْسَنَ الوضوءَ، خَرَجَت خَطَايَاهُ مِن جَسَدِهِ حَتَى تَخرُجُ مِن تَحت أظفارِه ".

The Messenger of Allah (ﷺ) said, "Whoever performs ablution and does it well, his sins will depart from his body, even from beneath his nails."

Riyad as-Salihin, hadith number 1026

قَالَ رَسُولُ اللهِ صَلَّى اللَّهُ عَلَيْهِ وَسَلَّمَ: " مَنْ لَزِمَ الِاسْتِغْفَارَ جَعَلَ اللَّهُ لَهُ مِنْ كُلِّ ضِيقٍ مَخْرَجًا ، وَمِنْ كُلِّ هَمٍّ فَرَجًا ، وَرَزَقَهُ مِنْ حَيْثُ لَا يَحْتَسِبُ ".

The Messenger of Allah (ﷺ) said, "Whoever adheres to seeking forgiveness, Allah will create an exit for him from every distress, and relief from every hardship, and will provide for him from sources he does not anticipate."

Riyad as-Salihin, Hadith number 1873

قَالَ رَسُولُ اللهِ صَلَّى اللَّهُ عَلَيْهِ وَسَلَّمَ: " إِنِّي لَأَسْتَغْفِرُ اللَّهَ وَأَتُوبُ إِلَيْهِ فِي الْيَوْمِ مِائَةَ مَرَّةٍ ".

The Messenger of Allah (ﷺ) said, "I seek Allah's forgiveness and turn to Him in repentance a hundred times a day."

Sunan Ibn Mayah, hadith number 3815

قَالَ رَسُولُ اللهِ صَلَّى اللَّهُ عَلَيْهِ وَسَلَّمَ: " مَنْ تَابَ قَبْلَ أَنْ تَطْلُعَ الشَّمْسُ مِنْ مَغْرِبِهَا تَابَ اللَّهُ عَلَيْهِ ".

The Messenger of Allah (ﷺ) said, "Whoever seeks repentance before the sun rises in the west, Allah will accept his repentance."

Sahih Muslim, hadith number 2703

HADITHS ON FORGIVENESS

قَالَ رَسُولُ اللَّهِ صَلَّى اللَّهُ عَلَيْهِ وَسَلَّمَ: " مَنْ قَامَ رَمَضَانَ إِيمَانًا وَاحْتِسَابًا غُفِرَ لَهُ مَا تَقَدَّمَ مِنْ ذَنْبِهِ وَمَنْ قَامَ لَيْلَةَ الْقَدْرِ إِيمَانًا وَاحْتِسَابًا غُفِرَ لَهُ مَا تَقَدَّمَ مِنْ ذَنْبِهِ ".

The Messenger of Allah (ﷺ) said, "Whoever performs the voluntary night prayer in Ramadan in faith and with the hope of reward, his previous sins will be forgiven. And whoever spends the night of Lailat Al Qadr in prayer in faith and in hope of reward, his previous sins will be forgiven."

Sunan Al-Nasa'i, hadith number 5027

قَالَ رَسُولُ اللَّهِ صَلَّى اللَّهُ عَلَيْهِ وَسَلَّمَ: " بَيْنَمَا رَجُلٌ يَمْشِي بِطَرِيقٍ وَجَدَ غُصْنَ شَوْكٍ عَلَى الطَّرِيقِ فَأَخَّرَهُ فَشَكَرَ اللَّهُ لَهُ فَغَفَرَ لَهُ ".

The Messenger of Allah (ﷺ) said, "If a man walks on a path, finds a thorny branch lying on the path and pushes it away, Allah will thank him and forgive him."

Sahih Muslim, hadith number 1914 b

قَالَ رَسُولُ اللَّهِ صَلَّى اللَّهُ عَلَيْهِ وَسَلَّمَ: " كَانَ الرَّجُلُ يُدَايِنُ النَّاسَ، فَكَانَ يَقُولُ لِفَتَاهُ إِذَا أَتَيْتَ مُعْسِرًا فَتَجَاوَزْ عَنْهُ، لَعَلَّ اللَّهَ أَنْ يَتَجَاوَزَ عَنَّا. قَالَ فَلَقِيَ اللَّهَ فَتَجَاوَزَ عَنْهُ ".

The Messenger of Allah (ﷺ) said, "There used to be a man who would lend money to the people, and he would instruct his servant: 'When someone is in difficulty and unable to repay, forgive him so that perhaps Allah will forgive us.' When he met Allah, Allah forgave him."

Sahih Al-Bukhari, hadith number 3480

HADITHS ON FORGIVENESS

قَالَ رَسُولُ اللَّهِ صَلَّى اللَّهُ عَلَيْهِ وَسَلَّمَ " مَا أَصَرَّ مَنِ اسْتَغْفَرَ وَلَوْ فَعَلَهُ فِي الْيَوْمِ سَبْعِينَ مَرَّةً ".

The Messenger of Allah (ﷺ) said, "Whoever asks
for forgiveness has not sinned grievously, even if
he has sinned seventy times in one day."

Sahih Al Tirmidhi, hadith number 3559

قَالَ رَسُولُ اللَّهِ صَلَّى اللَّهُ عَلَيْهِ وَسَلَّمَ " مَا مِنْ مُسْلِمَيْنِ يَلْتَقِيَانِ
فَيَتَصَافَحَانِ إِلاَّ غُفِرَ لَهُمَا قَبْلَ أَنْ يَفْتَرِقَا " .

The Prophet (ﷺ) said, "When two Muslims
meet and shake hands, their sins are forgiven
before they depart from each other."

Sunan Abu Dawûd, hadith number 5212

قَالَ رَسُولُ اللَّهِ صَلَّى اللَّهُ عَلَيْهِ وَسَلَّمَ " يَنْزِلُ رَبُّنَا كُلَّ لَيْلَةٍ إِلَى السَّمَاءِ الدُّنْيَا حِينَ يَبْقَى ثُلُثُ اللَّيْلِ
الآخِرُ فَيَقُولُ مَنْ يَدْعُونِي فَأَسْتَجِيبَ لَهُ وَمَنْ يَسْأَلُنِي فَأُعْطِيَهُ وَمَنْ يَسْتَغْفِرُنِي فَأَغْفِرَ لَهُ ".

The Messenger of Allah (ﷺ) said, "Our Lord descends
every night to the lower heaven at the last third of the
night and says, "Who calls upon Me that I may answer
him? Who asks Me that I may give him? And who
asks Me for forgiveness that I may forgive him?"

Sahih Al Tirmidhi, hadith number 3498

HADITHS ON FORGIVENESS

قَالَ رَسُولُ اللهِ صَلَّى اللهُ عَلَيْهِ وَسَلَّمَ " إِذَا تَوَضَّأَ الْعَبْدُ الْمُسْلِمُ – أَوِ الْمُؤْمِنُ – فَغَسَلَ وَجْهَهُ خَرَجَ مِنْ وَجْهِهِ كُلُّ خَطِيئَةٍ نَظَرَ إِلَيْهَا بِعَيْنَيْهِ مَعَ الْمَاءِ – أَوْ مَعَ آخِرِ قَطْرِ الْمَاءِ – فَإِذَا غَسَلَ يَدَيْهِ خَرَجَ مِنْ يَدَيْهِ كُلُّ خَطِيئَةٍ كَانَ بَطَشَتْهَا يَدَاهُ مَعَ الْمَاءِ – أَوْ مَعَ آخِرِ قَطْرِ الْمَاءِ – فَإِذَا غَسَلَ رِجْلَيْهِ خَرَجَتْ كُلُّ خَطِيئَةٍ مَشَتْهَا رِجْلَاهُ مَعَ الْمَاءِ – أَوْ مَعَ آخِرِ قَطْرِ الْمَاءِ – حَتَّى يَخْرُجَ نَقِيًّا مِنَ الذُّنُوبِ " .

The Messenger of Allah (ﷺ) said: "When a Muslim or believer performs ablution (wudu) and washes his face, every sin he looked at with his eyes comes out from his face with the water or with the last drop of water. When he washes his hands, every sin he committed with his hands comes out from his hands with the water or with the last drop of water. When he washes his feet, every sin to which his feet have walked comes out from his feet with the water or with the last drop of water, until he emerges cleansed from sins."

Sahih Muslim, hadith number 244

قَالَ رَسُولُ اللهِ صَلَّى اللهُ عَلَيْهِ وَسَلَّمَ " الصَّلَاةُ الْخَمْسُ وَالْجُمُعَةُ إِلَى الْجُمُعَةِ كَفَّارَةٌ لِمَا بَيْنَهُنَّ مَا لَمْ تُغْشَ الْكَبَائِرُ " .

The Messenger of Allah (ﷺ) said, "The five daily prayers and Friday prayer until the next Friday prayer are expiation for what occurs between them, as long as major sins are avoided."

Sahih Muslim, hadith number 233 a

HADITHS ON CHARACTER WEAKNESSES

قَالَ رَسُولُ اللهِ صَلَّى اللهُ عَلَيْهِ وَسَلَّمَ " آيَةُ الْمُنَافِقِ ثَلَاثٌ: إِذَا حَدَّثَ كَذَبَ، وَإِذَا وَعَدَ أَخْلَفَ، وَإِذَا أُوتُمِنَ خَانَ ".

The Messenger of Allah (ﷺ) said, "The signs of a hypocrite are three: Whenever he speaks, he tells a lie. Whenever he promises something, he breaks his promise. If you trust him, he proves to be dishonest. (If you trust him with something, he will not return it to you)."

Riyad as-Salihin, hadith number 199

إِنَّ رَسُولَ اللهِ صَلَّى اللهُ عَلَيْهِ وَسَلَّمَ قَالَ لَنَا " إِذَا غَضِبَ أَحَدُكُمْ وَهُوَ قَائِمٌ فَلْيَجْلِسْ فَإِنْ ذَهَبَ عَنْهُ الْغَضَبُ وَإِلاَّ فَلْيَضْطَجِعْ ".

The Messenger of Allah (ﷺ) told us, "When one of you gets angry while standing, let him sit down. If anger leaves him, it is well, otherwise let him lie down."

Sunan Abu Dawûd, hadith number 4782

قَالَ رَسُولُ اللهِ صَلَّى اللهُ عَلَيْهِ وَسَلَّمَ: " إِنَّ اللهَ جَمِيلٌ يُحِبُّ الْجَمَالَ، الْكِبْرُ بَطَرُ الْحَقِّ، وَغَمْطُ النَّاسِ".

The Prophet (ﷺ) said, "Allah is beautiful and loves beauty. Pride means denying the truth out of self-love and despising people."

Riyad as-Salihin, hadith number 1575

HADITHS ON CHARACTER
WEAKNESSES

قَالَ النَّبِيُّ صَلَّى اللهُ عَلَيْهِ وَسَلَّمَ: " أَفْرَى الْفِرَى أَنْ يُرِيَ الرجُلُ عَيْنَيْهِ مَا لَمْ تَرَيا " .

The Prophet (ﷺ) said, "The worst lie of all is to pretend that you have seen something you have not seen."

Riyad as-Salihin, hadith number 1545

قَالَ النَّبِيُّ صَلَّى اللهُ عَلَيْهِ وَسَلَّمَ " الْعَيْنُ حَقٌّ ". وَنَهَى عَنِ الْوَشْمِ.

The Prophet (ﷺ) said, "The effect of the evil eye is a fact." And he forbade tattoos.

Sahih Al-Bukhari, hadith number 5740

قَالَ رَسُولُ اللهِ صَلَّى اللهُ عَلَيْهِ وَسَلَّمَ " لاَ تُكْثِرُوا الْكَلاَمَ بِغَيْرِ ذِكْرِ اللهِ فَإِنَّ كَثْرَةَ الْكَلاَمِ بِغَيْرِ ذِكْرِ اللهِ قَسْوَةٌ لِلْقَلْبِ وَإِنَّ أَبْعَدَ النَّاسِ مِنَ اللهِ الْقَلْبُ الْقَاسِي " .

The Messenger of Allah (ﷺ) said, "Do not speak too much without remembering Allah. Talking too much without remembering Allah hardens the heart. And verily, he who is farthest from Allah is the hard-hearted."

Yam'a Al Tirmidhi, hadith number 2411

HADITHS ON CHARACTER WEAKNESSES

قَالَ رَسُولُ اللَّهِ صَلَّى اللَّهُ عَلَيْهِ وَسَلَّمَ " آيَةُ الْمُنَافِقِ ثَلَاثٌ إِذَا
حَدَّثَ كَذَبَ، وَإِذَا وَعَدَ أَخْلَفَ، وَإِذَا اؤْتُمِنَ خَانَ ".

The Prophet (ﷺ) said, "The signs of a hypocrite are three: Whenever he speaks, he tells a lie. Whenever he promises something, he breaks his promise. If you trust him, he proves to be dishonest. (If you trust him with something, he will not return it to you)."

Sahih Al-Bukhari, hadith number 33

قَالَ رَسُولُ اللَّهِ صَلَّى اللَّهُ عَلَيْهِ وَسَلَّمَ " إِنَّ مِنْ شَرِّ النَّاسِ ذَا
الْوَجْهَيْنِ الَّذِي يَأْتِي هَؤُلَاءِ بِوَجْهٍ وَهَؤُلَاءِ بِوَجْهٍ ".

The Messenger of Allah (ﷺ) said, "The worst of men is the two-faced; he appears to some with one face and to others with the other."

Sahih Muslim, hadith number 2526 c

قَالَ رَسُولُ اللَّهِ صَلَّى اللَّهُ عَلَيْهِ وَسَلَّمَ " مَنْ كَذَبَ عَلَيَّ مُتَعَمِّدًا فَلْيَتَبَوَّأْ مَقْعَدَهُ مِنَ النَّارِ ".

The Messenger of Allah (ﷺ) said, "Anyone who deliberately lies about me will certainly end up in Hell."

Sunan Abu Dawûd, hadith number 3651

HADITHS ON CHARACTER WEAKNESSES

قَالَ رَسُولُ اللهِ صَلَّى اللهُ عَلَيْهِ وَسَلَّمَ " لاَ تَلاَعَنُوا بِلَعْنَةِ اللهِ وَلاَ بِغَضَبِ اللهِ وَلاَ بِالنَّارِ " .

The Prophet (ﷺ) said, "Do not curse one another with the curse of Allah, nor with His anger, nor with the Fire."

Sunan Abu Dawûd, hadith number 4906

قَالَ رَسُولُ اللهِ صَلَّى اللهُ عَلَيْهِ وَسَلَّمَ " الْمُؤْمِنُ غِرٌّ كَرِيمٌ وَالْفَاجِرُ خِبٌّ لَئِيمٌ " .

The Prophet (ﷺ) said, "The believer is noble and generous, but the vicious is deceitful and corrupt."

Sunan Abu Dawûd, hadith number 4790

قَالَ رَسُولُ اللهِ صَلَّى اللهُ عَلَيْهِ وَسَلَّمَ " مَنْ لاَ يَرْحَم النَّاسَ لاَ يَرْحَمْهُ اللهُ عَزَّ وَجَلَّ " .

The Messenger of Allah (ﷺ) said, "Whoever does not show mercy to people, Allah, Exalted and Glorious, does not show mercy to him."

Sahih Muslim, hadith number 2319 a

قَالَ رَسُولُ اللهِ صَلَّى اللهُ عَلَيْهِ وَسَلَّمَ " هَلَكَ الْمُتَنَطِّعُونَ " . قَالَهَا ثَلاَثًا .

The Messenger of Allah (ﷺ) said, "Those who are excessively disobedient have perished." He repeated this three times."

Sahih Muslim, hadith number 2670

HADITHS ON CHARACTER WEAKNESSES

عَنِ النَّبِيِّ صَلَّى اللهُ عَلَيْهِ وَسَلَّمَ قَالَ " إِيَّاكُمْ وَالظَّنَّ، فَإِنَّ الظَّنَّ أَكْذَبُ الْحَدِيثِ، وَلاَ تَجَسَّسُوا، وَلاَ تَحَسَّسُوا، وَلاَ تَبَاغَضُوا، وَكُونُوا إِخْوَانًا ". وَلاَ يَخْطُبُ الرَّجُلُ عَلَى خِطْبَةِ أَخِيهِ حَتَّى يَنْكِحَ أَوْ يَتْرُكَ ".

The Prophet (ﷺ) said, "Beware of suspicion (against one another), for suspicions are the most false talk, and do not spy on one another, and do not listen to people's maledictions about one another's affairs, and do not be hostile to one another, but be brothers. And let no one ask for the hand of a girl who is already betrothed to his (Muslim) brother, but wait until he marries her or leaves her."

Sahih Al-Bukhari, hadith number 5143, 5144

قَالَ رَسُولُ اللهِ صَلَّى اللهُ عَلَيْهِ وَسَلَّمَ: " لا يَرْمِي رَجُلٌ رَجُلًا بِالْفِسْقِ أَو الْكُفْرِ إِلا ارْتَدَّتْ عَلَيْهِ، إن لم يَكُنْ صَاحِبه كذلك ".

The Messenger of Allah (ﷺ) said, "If a Muslim accuses another of sin or disbelief, the accusation falls on the person who uttered it if the other person does not deserve it."

Riyad as-Salihin, hadith number 1560

عَنْ حُذَيْفَةَ، قَالَ قَالَ رَسُولُ اللهِ صَلَّى اللهُ عَلَيْهِ وَسَلَّمَ " لاَ يَدْخُلُ الْجَنَّةَ قَتَّاتٌ ".

Hudhayfah related that the Messenger of Allah (ﷺ) said, "A slanderer will not enter Paradise."

Sunan Abu Dawûd, hadith number 4871

HADITHS ON CHARACTER WEAKNESSES

قَالَ رَسُولُ الله صَلَّ اللهُ عَلَيْهِ وَسَلَّمَ : " يا نِساءَ المُسْلِماتِ،
لا تَحْقِرَنَّ جارَةٌ لِجارَتِها، ولو فِرْسِنَ شاةٍ ".

The Messenger of Allah (ﷺ) said, "O Muslim
women, never despise a gift given to you by your
neighbor, even if it is the hoof of a sheep."

Riyad as-Salihin, hadith number 124

عَنِ ابْنِ عَبَّاسٍ قَالَ: قَالَ رَسُولُ اللهِ صَلَّى اللهُ عَلَيْهِ وَسَلَّمَ: " عَلِّمُوا وَيَسِّرُوا،
عَلِّمُوا وَيَسِّرُوا، ثَلَاثَ مَرَّاتٍ، وَإِذَا غَضِبْتَ فَاسْكُتْ، مَرَّتَيْنِ ".

Ibn 'Abbas said, "The Prophet (ﷺ) said, "Teach and make it
easy. Teach and make it easy. Teach and make it easy." three
times. And he added twice: "If you are angry, be quiet."

Al Adab Al Mufrad, hadith number 1320

عَنْ أَبِي هُرَيْرَةَ، رَضِي اللهُ عنه، أَنَّ رَجُلًا قَالَ لِلنَّبِيِّ ﷺ: أَوْصِنِي،
قَالَ: " لا تَغْضَب، فَرَدَّدَ مِرَارًا قَالَ: لا تَغْضَبْ ".

Abu Huraira (may Allah be pleased with him) related that a man
asked the Prophet (ﷺ) for advice and the Prophet (ﷺ) said, "Do
not get angry." The man repeated the question several times
and the Prophet (ﷺ) replied again and again, "Do not get angry."

Riyad as-Salihin, hadith number 48

HADITHS ON THE RELIEF OF PAIN AND SICKNESS

قَالَ رَسُولُ اللهِ صَلَّى اللهُ عَلَيْهِ وَسَلَّمَ " أَطْعِمُوا الْجَائِعَ، وَعُودُوا الْمَرِيضَ، وَفُكُّوا الْعَانِيَ ".

The Prophet (ﷺ) said, "Feed the hungry, visit the sick, and set the captive free."

Sahih Al-Bukhari, hadith number 5649

[...] سَمِعْتُ رَسُولَ اللهِ صَلَّى اللهُ عَلَيْهِ وَسَلَّمَ يَقُولُ " لَا يَمُوتَنَّ أَحَدٌ مِنْكُمْ إِلاَّ وَهُوَ يُحْسِنُ الظَّنَّ بِاللهِ ".

[...] I heard Allah's Messenger (ﷺ) say, "May none of you die without thinking favorably of Allah."

Sunan Ibn Mayah, hadith number 4167

سُئِلَ رَسُولُ اللهِ صَلَّى اللهُ عَلَيْهِ وَسَلَّمَ عَنِ النُّشْرَةِ فَقَالَ " هُوَ مِنْ عَمَلِ الشَّيْطَانِ ".

The Messenger of Allah (ﷺ) was asked about a remedy for a possessed person (nushrah). He replied, "It is the work of the devil."

Sunan Abu Dawûd, hadith number 3868

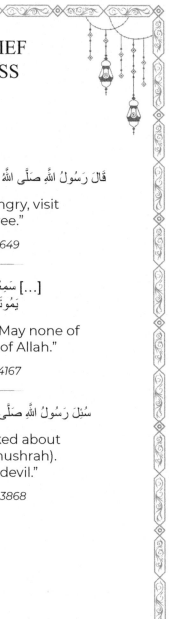

HADITHS ON THE RELIEF OF PAIN AND SICKNESS

قَالَ رَسُولُ اللَّهِ صَلَّى اللَّهُ عَلَيْهِ وَسَلَّمَ " إِذَا سَمِعْتُمْ بِالطَّاعُونِ بِأَرْضٍ فَلَا تَدْخُلُوهَا، وَإِذَا وَقَعَ بِأَرْضٍ وَأَنْتُمْ بِهَا فَلَا تَخْرُجُوا مِنْهَا ".

The Prophet (ﷺ) said, "If you hear of the outbreak of a pandemic in a country, do not enter it; but if the pandemic breaks out in a place while you are there, do not leave that place."

Sahih Al-Bukhari, hadith number 5728

قَالَ رَسُولُ اللَّهِ صَلَّى اللَّهُ عَلَيْهِ وَسَلَّمَ " إِذَا وَقَعَ الذُّبَابُ فِي إِنَاءِ أَحَدِكُمْ، فَلْيَغْمِسْهُ كُلَّهُ، ثُمَّ لْيَطْرَحْهُ، فَإِنَّ فِي أَحَدِ جَنَاحَيْهِ شِفَاءً وَفِي الْآخَرِ دَاءً ".

The Messenger of Allah (ﷺ) said, "If a fly falls into the bowl, immerse it completely (in the bowl) and only then throw it away, for in one of its wings is a disease and in the other is the cure (the antidote for it)."

Sahih Al-Bukhari, hadith number 5782

قَالَ رَسُولُ اللَّهِ صَلَّى اللَّهُ عَلَيْهِ وَسَلَّمَ " مَا أَنْزَلَ اللَّهُ دَاءً إِلَّا أَنْزَلَ لَهُ شِفَاءً ".

The Prophet (ﷺ) said, "There is no disease that Allah has created without also creating the cure."

Sahih Al-Bukhari, hadith number 5678

HADITHS ON THE RELIEF OF PAIN AND SICKNESS

نَهَى رَسُولُ اللهِ صَلَّى اللهُ عَلَيْهِ وَسَلَّمَ عَنِ الدَّوَاءِ الْخَبِيثِ .

The Messenger of Allah (ﷺ) forbade impure medicine.

Sunan Abu Dawûd, hadith number 3870

قَالَ رَسُولُ اللهِ صَلَّى اللهُ عَلَيْهِ وَسَلَّمَ " مَا مِنْ مُسْلِمٍ يُصِيبُهُ أَذًى
إِلاَّ حَاتَّتْ عَنْهُ خَطَايَاهُ كَمَا تَحَاتُ وَرَقُ الشَّجَرِ ".

The Prophet (ﷺ) said, "No Muslim will be afflicted by a disease without his sins being wiped out, like the leaves falling from a tree."

Sahih Al-Bukhari, hadith number 5661

قَالَ رَسُولُ اللهِ صَلَّى اللهُ عَلَيْهِ وَسَلَّمَ " إِنَّ فِيهِ (الْحِجَامَةِ مِنَ الدَّاءِ) شِفَاءً ".

The Prophet (ﷺ) said, "Cupping heals."

Sahih Al-Bukhari, hadith number 5697

قَالَ رَسُولُ اللهِ صَلَّى اللهُ عَلَيْهِ وَسَلَّمَ " إِنَّ هَذِهِ الْحَبَّةَ السَّوْدَاءَ
شِفَاءٌ مِنْ كُلِّ دَاءٍ إِلاَّ مِنَ السَّامِ (الْمَوْتُ) ".

The Prophet (ﷺ) said, "Black cumin is curative for all diseases except death."

Sahih Al-Bukhari, hadith number 5687

HADITHS ON THE RELIEF
OF PAIN AND SICKNESS

قَالَ رَسُولُ اللَّهِ صَلَّى اللَّهُ عَلَيْهِ وَسَلَّمَ " الْكَمْأَةُ مِنَ الْمَنِّ ((أي أنها تنمو بشكل طبيعي دون رعاية الإنسان)، وَمَاؤُهَا شِفَاءٌ لِلْعَيْنِ ".

The Prophet (ﷺ) said, "Truffles are like manna
(i.e., they grow naturally without man's care)
and their water cures eye diseases."

Sahih Al-Bukhari, hadith number 5708

عَنِ عبد الله بْنِ عُمَرَ ـ رضى الله عنهما ـ عَنِ النَّبِيِّ صَلَّى اللَّهُ عَلَيْهِ وَسَلَّمَ قَالَ " الْحُمَّى مِنْ فَيْحِ جَهَنَّمَ فَأَطْفِئُوهَا بِالْمَاءِ ".

`Abdullah bin `Umar reported, "The Prophet (ﷺ) said,
"Fever comes from the heat of Hell, so cool it with water."

Sahih Al-Bukhari, hadith number 5723

قَالَ رَسُولُ اللَّهِ صَلَّى اللَّهُ عَلَيْهِ وَسَلَّمَ: " لا يَتَمَنَّيَنَّ أَحَدُكُمُ الْمَوْتَ مِن ضُرٍّ أَصَابَهُ، فإنْ كانَ لا بُدَّ فاعِلًا، فَلْيَقُلِ: اللَّهُمَّ أَحْيِنِي ما كانَتِ الْحَياةُ خَيْرًا لِي، وتَوَفَّنِي إذا كانَتِ الْوَفاةُ خَيْرًا لِي".

The Messenger of Allah (ﷺ) said, "None of you should desire
death because of a calamity befalling him. If he cannot help
it, he should say: ‹O Allah, let me live as long as you know that
life is better for me, and let me die if death is better for me.'

Riyad as-Salihin, hadith number 40

104

HADITHS ON THE RELIEF
OF PAIN AND SICKNESS

قَالَ رَسُولُ اللهِ صَلَّى اللهُ عَلَيْهِ وَسَلَّمَ " لاَ يَتَمَنَّيَنَّ أَحَدٌ مِنْكُمُ الْمَوْتَ إِمَّا
مُحْسِنًا فَلَعَلَّهُ أَنْ يَزْدَادَ خَيْرًا وَإِمَّا مُسِيئًا فَلَعَلَّهُ أَنْ يَسْتَعْتِبَ " .

The Messenger of Allah (ﷺ) said, "None of you should wish
for death. Either he is a doer of good deeds and may add
to them, or he is an evildoer but perhaps he may stop."

Sunan Al-Nasa'i, hadith number 1818

قَالَ رَسُولُ اللهِ صَلَّى اللهُ عَلَيْهِ وَسَلَّمَ: " إِذَا مَرِضَ العَبْدُ أَو سَافَرَ
كُتِبَ لَهُ مِنَ العَمَلِ مَا كَانَ يَعْمَلُهُ وَهُوَ صَحِيحٌ مُقِيمٌ " .

The Messenger of Allah (ﷺ) said, "If a servant of Allah falls sick or
goes on a journey, he will be credited with the same good deeds
that he would have done had he been healthy or at home."

Riyad as-Salihin, hadith number 133

قَالَ رَسُولُ اللهِ صَلَّى اللهُ عَلَيْهِ وَسَلَّمَ " الشِّفَاءُ فِي ثَلاَثَةٍ شَرْبَةِ عَسَلٍ،
وَشَرْطَةِ مِحْجَمٍ، وَكَيَّةِ نَارٍ، وَأَنْهَى أُمَّتِي عَنِ الْكَيِّ " .

The Prophet (ﷺ) said, "Healing consists of three
things: a sip of honey, cupping and burning with fire
(cauterizing). But I forbid my followers to cauterize."

Sahih Al-Bukhari, hadith number 5680

HADITHS ON THE RELIEF
OF PAIN AND SICKNESS

عَنْ عَائِشَةَ، قَالَتْ كَانَ رَسُولُ اللَّهِ صَلَّى اللَّهُ عَلَيْهِ وَسَلَّمَ إِذَا أَخَذَ أَهْلَهُ الْوَعْكُ
أَمَرَ بِالْحَسَاءِ فَصُنِعَ ثُمَّ أَمَرَهُمْ فَحَسَوْا مِنْهُ وَكَانَ يَقُولُ " إِنَّهُ لَيَرْتُو فُؤَادَ الْحَزِينِ
وَيَسْرُو عَنْ فُؤَادِ السَّقِيمِ كَمَا تَسْرُو إِحْدَاكُنَّ الْوَسَخَ بِالْمَاءِ عَنْ وَجْهِهَا " .

Aisha narrated, "When one of the wives of the Messenger
of Allah (ﷺ) fell sick (feverishly), he would order soup to be
prepared for her. Then he would invite her to drink some of
the soup. And he would say, "It strengthens the heart of the
afflicted and removes sadness from the heart of the sick,
just as one of you removes dirt from her face with water."

Sahih Al Tirmidhi, hadith number 2039

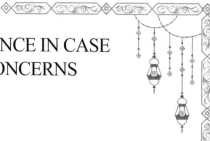

HADITHS ON ASSISTANCE IN CASE OF NEEDS AND CONCERNS

عَنْ أَنَسِ بْنِ مَالِكٍ، قَالَ قَالَ رَسُولُ اللَّهِ صَلَّى اللَّهُ عَلَيْهِ وَسَلَّمَ " يَأْتِي عَلَى النَّاسِ زَمَانٌ الصَّابِرُ فِيهِمْ عَلَى دِينِهِ كَالْقَابِضِ عَلَى الْجَمْرِ " .

Anas bin Malik narrated that the Messenger of Allah (ﷺ) said, "A time will come to the people when the one who is patient with his religion will be like the one who holds a burning ember."

Yam'a Al Tirmidhi, hadith number 2260

عَنْ عَبْدِ اللَّهِ بْنِ عَمْرٍو، قَالَ قَالَ رَسُولُ اللَّهِ صَلَّى اللَّهُ عَلَيْهِ وَسَلَّمَ " مَنْ صَمَتَ نَجَا " .

'Abdullah bin 'Amr related that the Messenger of Allah (ﷺ) said, "Whoever keeps silent saves himself."

Yam'a Al Tirmidhi, hadith number 2501

قَالَ رَسُولُ اللَّهِ صَلَّى اللَّهُ عَلَيْهِ وَسَلَّمَ " مَنْ يُرِدِ اللَّهُ بِهِ خَيْرًا يُصِبْ مِنْهُ " .

The Messenger of Allah (ﷺ) said, "When Allah wants to do something good for someone, He puts him to the test."

Sahih Al-Bukhari, hadith number 5645

HADITHS ON ASSISTANCE IN CASE
OF NEEDS AND CONCERNS

قَالَ رَسُولُ اللهِ صَلَّى اللهُ عَلَيْهِ وَسَلَّمَ " وَتُغِيثُوا الْمَلْهُوفَ وَتَهْدُوا الضَّالَّ " .

The Prophet (ﷺ) said, "And provide support to
the needy and guide the one who is lost."

Sunan Abu Dawûd, hadith number 4817

عَنِ النَّبِيِّ ـ صلى الله عليه وسلم ـ فِي قَوْلِهِ تَعَالَى {كُلَّ يَوْم هُوَ فِي شَأْنٍ} . قَالَ
" مِنْ شَأْنِهِ أَنْ يَغْفِرَ ذَنْبًا وَيُفَرِّجَ كَرْبًا وَيَرْفَعَ قَوْمًا وَيَخْفِضَ آخَرِينَ " .

The Prophet (ﷺ) said about this verse [Every day He is involved
in some affair], "His affairs include forgiving sins, relieving
hardships, exalting some people and humiliating others."

Sunan Ibn Mayah, hadith number 202

قَالَ رَسُولُ اللهِ صَلَّى اللهُ عَلَيْهِ وَسَلَّمَ " مَا يُصِيبُ الْمُؤْمِنَ مِنْ وَصَبٍ وَلاَ
نَصَبٍ وَلاَ سَقَمٍ وَلاَ حَزَنٍ حَتَّى الْهَمَّ يُهَمُّهُ إِلاَّ كُفِّرَ بِهِ مِنْ سَيِّئَاتِهِ " .

The Messenger of Allah (ﷺ) said, "No fatigue, illness,
anxiety, sorrow, harm, or sadness afflicts any Muslim,
without Allah wiping out his sins by it."

Sahih Muslim, hadith number 2573

HADITHS ON ASSISTANCE IN CASE OF NEEDS AND CONCERNS

عَنْ عَبْدِ اللَّهِ بْنِ مَسْعُودٍ، قَالَ قَالَ رَسُولُ اللَّهِ صَلَّى اللَّهُ عَلَيْهِ وَسَلَّمَ " مَنْ نَزَلَتْ بِهِ فَاقَةٌ فَأَنْزَلَهَا بِالنَّاسِ لَمْ تُسَدَّ فَاقَتُهُ وَمَنْ نَزَلَتْ بِهِ فَاقَةٌ فَأَنْزَلَهَا بِاللَّهِ فَيُوشِكُ اللَّهُ لَهُ بِرِزْقٍ عَاجِلٍ أَوْ آجِلٍ " .

Abdullah bin Mas'ud narrated that the Messenger of Allah (ﷺ) said: "Whoever suffers hardship and supplicates to people, his hardship will not end. And whoever suffers hardship and supplicates to Allah, sooner or later Allah will grant him something".

Sahih Al Tirmidhi, hadith number 2326

قَالَ رَسُولُ اللَّهِ صَلَّى اللَّهُ عَلَيْهِ وَسَلَّمَ " مَنْ تَرَكَ مَالاً فَلأَهْلِهِ وَمَنْ تَرَكَ ضَيَاعًا فَإِلَيَّ " .

The Messenger of Allah (ﷺ) said "Whoever leaves wealth, it is for his heirs, and whoever leaves poor relatives, it (the responsibility) is for me."

Yam'a Al Tirmidhi, hadith number 2090

HADITHS ON ASSISTANCE IN CASE OF NEEDS AND CONCERNS

عَنْ أَنَسٍ، قَالَ قَالَ رَسُولُ اللَّهِ صَلَّى اللَّهُ عَلَيْهِ وَسَلَّمَ " إِذَا أَرَادَ اللَّهُ بِعَبْدِهِ الْخَيْرَ عَجَّلَ لَهُ الْعُقُوبَةَ فِي الدُّنْيَا وَإِذَا أَرَادَ اللَّهُ بِعَبْدِهِ الشَّرَّ أَمْسَكَ عَنْهُ بِذَنْبِهِ حَتَّى يُوَفَّى بِهِ يَوْمَ الْقِيَامَةِ " . [...] إِنَّ عِظَمَ الْجَزَاءِ مَعَ عِظَمِ الْبَلاَءِ وَإِنَّ اللَّهَ إِذَا أَحَبَّ قَوْمًا ابْتَلاَهُمْ فَمَنْ رَضِيَ فَلَهُ الرِّضَا وَمَنْ سَخِطَ فَلَهُ السَّخَطُ " .

Anas narrated that the Messenger of Allah (ﷺ) said, "When Allah wills good for His servant, He hastens his punishment in this world. And when He wills evil for His servant, He conceals his sins from him until he appears before Him on the Day of Resurrection. [Surely, a greater reward is accompanied by a greater trial. And verily, when Allah loves a people, He tests them. So whom He pleases, He pleases, and whom He displeases, He angers."

Sahih Al Tirmidhi, hadith number 2396

قَالَ رَسُولُ اللَّهِ صَلَّى اللَّهُ عَلَيْهِ وَسَلَّمَ " مَنْ قَعَدَ مَقْعَدًا لَمْ يَذْكُرِ اللَّهَ فِيهِ كَانَتْ عَلَيْهِ مِنَ اللَّهِ تِرَةً وَمَنِ اضْطَجَعَ مَضْجَعًا لاَ يَذْكُرُ اللَّهَ فِيهِ كَانَتْ عَلَيْهِ مِنَ اللَّهِ تِرَةً " .

The Prophet (ﷺ) said, "Whoever sits in a place and does not mention Allah, upon him is a woe from Allah; and whoever lies down and does not mention Allah, upon him is a woe from Allah."

Sunan Abu Dawûd, hadith number 4856

HADITHS ON SUPPORT

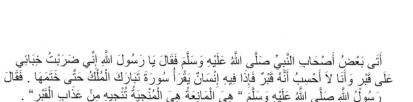

أَتَى بَعْضُ أَصْحَابِ النَّبِيِّ صَلَّى اللَّهُ عَلَيْهِ وَسَلَّمَ فَقَالَ يَا رَسُولَ اللَّهِ إِنِّي ضَرَبْتُ خِبَائِي عَلَى قَبْرٍ وَأَنَا لاَ أَحْسِبُ أَنَّهُ قَبْرٌ فَإِذَا فِيهِ إِنْسَانٌ يَقْرَأُ سُورَةَ تَبَارَكَ الْمُلْكُ حَتَّى خَتَمَهَا . فَقَالَ رَسُولُ اللَّهِ صَلَّى اللَّهُ عَلَيْهِ وَسَلَّمَ " هِيَ الْمَانِعَةُ هِيَ الْمُنْجِيَةُ تُنْجِيهِ مِنْ عَذَابِ الْقَبْرِ " .

One of the Companions went to the Prophet (ﷺ) and said to him, ‹O Messenger of Allah, I pitched my tent over a grave without realizing that it was a grave. Suddenly, I heard a person reciting Surah al-Mulk from the grave until he finished reading it. The Messenger of Allah (ﷺ) said, 'It is the Protector, It is the Deliverer, It delivers from the punishment of the grave.'

Yam'a Al Tirmidhi, hadith number 2890

قَالَ رَسُولُ اللَّهِ صَلَّى اللَّهُ عَلَيْهِ وَسَلَّمَ " ثَلاَثُ دَعَوَاتٍ يُسْتَجَابُ لَهُنَّ لاَ شَكَّ فِيهِنَّ دَعْوَةُ الْمَظْلُومِ وَدَعْوَةُ الْمُسَافِرِ وَدَعْوَةُ الْوَالِدِ لِوَلَدِهِ".

The Messenger of Allah (ﷺ) said, "There are three supplications that will certainly be answered: the supplication of the one who has been wronged, the supplication of the traveler, and the supplication of a parent for his/her son/daughter."

Sunan Ibn Mayah, hadith number 3862

HADITHS ON SUPPORT

قَالَ رَسُولُ اللهِ صَلَّى اللهُ عَلَيْهِ وَسَلَّمَ: " أَمَّا بَعْدُ، أَلَا أَيُّهَا النَّاسُ، فَإِنَّمَا أَنَا بَشَرٌ يُوشِكُ أَنْ
يَأْتِيَ رَسُولُ رَبِّي فَأُجِيبَ، وَأَنَا تَارِكٌ فِيكُمْ ثَقَلَيْنِ: أَوَّلُهُمَا كِتَابُ اللهِ، فِيهِ الْهُدَى وَالنُّورُ،
فَخُذُوا بِكِتَابِ اللهِ، وَاسْتَمْسِكُوا بِهِ، فَحَثَّ عَلَى كِتَابِ اللهِ وَرَغَّبَ فِيهِ، ثُمَّ قَالَ: وَأَهْلُ بَيْتِي،
أُذَكِّرُكُمُ اللهَ فِي أَهْلِ بَيْتِي، أُذَكِّرُكُمُ اللهَ فِي أَهْلِ بَيْتِي، أُذَكِّرُكُمُ اللهَ فِي أَهْلِ بَيْتِي ".

The Prophet (ﷺ) said, "O people, I am a human being. I am
about to receive a messenger (the Angel of Death), and I will
answer the call of Allah, but I leave you two weighty things:
the first is the Book of Allah, which contains guidance and
light, so cling to the Quran." He exhorted us to cling to the
Quran and then said, "The second is the members of my
family, I remind you to be kind to the members of my family."

Riyad as-Salihin, hadith number 346

يَقُولُ عُمَرُ سَمِعْتُ رَسُولَ اللهِ صَلَّى اللهُ عَلَيْهِ وَسَلَّمَ يَقُولُ " لَوْ أَنَّكُمْ تَوَكَّلْتُمْ عَلَى
اللهِ حَقَّ تَوَكُّلِهِ لَرَزَقَكُمْ كَمَا يَرْزُقُ الطَّيْرَ تَغْدُو خِمَاصًا وَتَرُوحُ بِطَانًا " .

'Umar said, "I heard Allah's Messenger (ﷺ) say, "If you
trust in Allah as you should, you would provide for
yourselves like the birds: they go out hungry in the
morning and return in the evening with full bellies."

Sunan Ibn Mayah, hadith number 4164

HADITHS ON SUPPORT

عَنْ أَبِي مُوسَى، قَالَ قَالَ رَسُولُ اللهِ صَلَّى اللهُ عَلَيْهِ وَسَلَّمَ "
الْمُؤْمِنُ لِلْمُؤْمِنِ كَالْبُنْيَانِ يَشُدُّ بَعْضُهُ بَعْضًا " .

Abu Musa related that the Messenger of Allah
(ﷺ) said, "A believer is like a brick to another
believer, one supports the other."

Sahih Muslim, hadith number 2585

قَالَ رَسُولُ اللهِ صَلَّى اللهُ عَلَيْهِ وَسَلَّمَ " مَنْ سَرَّهُ أَنْ يَسْتَجِيبَ اللهُ لَهُ
عِنْدَ الشَّدَائِدِ وَالْكَرَبِ فَلْيُكْثِرِ الدُّعَاءَ فِي الرَّخَاءِ " .

The Messenger of Allah (ﷺ) said, "Whoever is pleased that
Allah would respond to him during adversity and hardship,
let him increase his supplication during times of ease."

Sahih Al Tirmidhi, hadith number 3382

قَالَ رَسُولُ اللهِ صَلَّى اللهُ عَلَيْهِ وَسَلَّمَ " مَنْ كَانَتِ الدُّنْيَا هَمَّهُ فَرَّقَ اللهُ عَلَيْهِ أَمْرَهُ وَجَعَلَ فَقْرَهُ بَيْنَ عَيْنَيْهِ وَلَمْ يَأْتِهِ مِنَ الدُّنْيَا إِلاَّ مَا كُتِبَ لَهُ وَمَنْ كَانَتِ الآخِرَةُ نِيَّتَهُ جَمَعَ اللهُ لَهُ أَمْرَهُ وَجَعَلَ غِنَاهُ فِي قَلْبِهِ وَأَتَتْهُ الدُّنْيَا وَهِيَ رَاغِمَةٌ " .

The Messenger of Allah (ﷺ) said, "Whoever makes the world
his most important matter, Allah will confound his affairs
and make poverty appear before his eyes, and he will not get
anything from the world except what has been decreed for him.
But whoever makes the Hereafter his most important matter,
Allah will settle his affairs and make him content in his heart,
and the world will come to him whether it wants to or not."

Sunan Ibn Mayah, hadith number 4105

HADITHS ON SUPPORT

قَالَ رَسُولُ اللَّهِ صَلَّى اللَّهُ عَلَيْهِ وَسَلَّمَ " [...] وَلْيَنْصُرِ الرَّجُلُ أَخَاهُ ظَالِمًا أَوْ مَظْلُومًا إِنْ كَانَ ظَالِمًا فَلْيَنْهَهُ فَإِنَّهُ لَهُ نَصْرٌ وَإِنْ كَانَ مَظْلُومًا فَلْيَنْصُرْهُ " .

The Messenger of Allah (ﷺ) said: " [...] A person should help his brother, whether he is an oppressor or an oppressed. If he is the oppressor, he should prevent him, for that is his help; and if he is the oppressed, he should help him against oppression."

Sahih Muslim, hadith number 2584 a

قَالَ رَسُولُ اللَّهِ صَلَّى اللَّهُ عَلَيْهِ وَسَلَّمَ " الْمُسْلِمُ أَخُو الْمُسْلِمِ لاَ يَظْلِمُهُ وَلاَ يُسْلِمُهُ مَنْ كَانَ فِي حَاجَةِ أَخِيهِ فَإِنَّ اللَّهَ فِي حَاجَتِهِ وَمَنْ فَرَّجَ عَنْ مُسْلِمٍ كُرْبَةً فَرَّجَ اللَّهُ عَنْهُ بِهَا كُرْبَةً مِنْ كُرَبِ يَوْمِ الْقِيَامَةِ وَمَنْ سَتَرَ مُسْلِمًا سَتَرَهُ اللَّهُ يَوْمَ الْقِيَامَةِ " .

The Messenger of Allah (ﷺ) said, "A Muslim is a brother to another Muslim; he neither wrongs him nor does he forsake him when he is in need; whoever fulfills the needs of his brother, Allah will fulfill his needs; whoever relieves a Muslim of distress, Allah will relieve him of distress on the Day of Judgment; and whoever covers up the faults of a Muslim, Allah will cover up his faults on the Day of Judgment."

Sunan Abu Dawûd, hadith number 4893

HADITHS ON SUPPORT

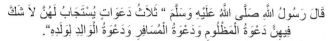

قَالَ رَسُولُ اللهِ صَلَّى اللهُ عَلَيْهِ وَسَلَّمَ " ثَلَاثُ دَعَوَاتٍ يُسْتَجَابُ لَهُنَّ لاَ شَكَّ فِيهِنَّ دَعْوَةُ الْمَظْلُومِ وَدَعْوَةُ الْمُسَافِرِ وَدَعْوَةُ الْوَالِدِ لِوَلَدِهِ".

The Messenger of Allah (ﷺ) said, "There are three supplications that will certainly be answered: the supplication of the one who has been wronged, the supplication of the traveler, and the supplication of a parent for his/her son/daughter."

Sunan Ibn Mayah, hadith number 3862

عَنْ ثَابِتٍ الْبُنَانِيِّ، أَنَّ رَسُولَ اللهِ صَلَّى اللهِ عَلَيْهِ وَسَلَّمَ قَالَ " لِيَسْأَلْ أَحَدُكُمْ رَبَّهُ حَاجَتَهُ حَتَّى يَسْأَلَهُ الْمِلْحَ وَحَتَّى يَسْأَلَهُ شِسْعَ نَعْلِهِ إِذَا انْقَطَعَ ".

Thabit Al-Bunani narrated that the Messenger of Allah (ﷺ) said, "You should ask your Lord for whatever you need, even if it is only salt or the strap of a sandal when it breaks."

Sahih Al Tirmidhi, hadith number 3604 j

عَنْ أَبِي الدَّرْدَاءِ، قَالَ قَالَ رَسُولُ اللهِ صَلَّى اللهُ عَلَيْهِ وَسَلَّمَ " مَا مِنْ عَبْدٍ مُسْلِمٍ يَدْعُو لأَخِيهِ بِظَهْرِ الْغَيْبِ إِلاَّ قَالَ الْمَلَكُ وَلَكَ بِمِثْلٍ " .

Abu al-Dardáa related that the Messenger of Allah (ﷺ) said, "No Muslim servant supplicates for his brother behind his back (in his absence) but that the angel says: 'Amin, and for you the same.'"

Sahih Muslim, hadith number 2732 a

HADITHS ON SUPPORT

قَالَ رَسُولُ اللهِ صَلَّى اللهُ عَلَيْهِ وَسَلَّمَ " يُسْتَجَابُ لِأَحَدِكُمْ مَا لَمْ يَعْجَلْ فَيَقُولُ قَدْ دَعَوْتُ فَلَا أَوْ فَلَمْ يُسْتَجَبْ لِي " .

The Messenger of Allah (ﷺ) said, "The supplication of every one of you will be answered if he does not become impatient and say, ‹I have prayed but I have not been answered.›

Sahih Muslim, hadith number 2735 a

سَمِعْتُ رَسُولَ اللهِ صَلَّى اللهُ عَلَيْهِ وَسَلَّمَ يَقُولُ " مَنْ سَرَّهُ أَنْ يُبْسَطَ عَلَيْهِ رِزْقُهُ أَوْ يُنْسَأَ فِي أَثَرِهِ فَلْيَصِلْ رَحِمَهُ " .

I heard the Messenger of Allah (ﷺ) say, "Whoever desires to have his means of livelihood extended or his age prolonged, let him keep good relations with his."

Sahih Muslim, hadith number 2557 a

قَالَ رَسُولُ اللهِ صَلَّى اللهُ عَلَيْهِ وَسَلَّمَ " الْمُؤْمِنُ الْقَوِيُّ خَيْرٌ وَأَحَبُّ إِلَى اللهِ مِنَ الْمُؤْمِنِ الضَّعِيفِ وَفِي كُلٍّ خَيْرٌ احْرِصْ عَلَى مَا يَنْفَعُكَ وَلَا تَعْجِزْ فَإِنْ غَلَبَكَ أَمْرٌ فَقُلْ قَدَّرَ اللهُ وَمَا شَاءَ فَعَلَ وَإِيَّاكَ وَاللَّوْ فَإِنَّ اللَّوْ تَفْتَحُ عَمَلَ الشَّيْطَانِ " .

The Messenger of Allah (ﷺ) said,"The strong believer is better and more beloved to Allah than the weak believer, while there is good in both. Guard over that which benefits you, seek help from Allah, and do not give up. If something afflicts you, do not say, 'If only I had done such and such.' Rather, say, 'Allah has decreed and what He wills, He does.' Verily, the phrase 'if only' opens the door for the deeds of Satan."

Sunan Ibn Mayah, hadith number 4168

HADITHS ON THE
FAMILY AND MARRIED LIFE

قَالَ رَسُولُ اللهِ صَلَّى اللهُ عَلَيْهِ وَسَلَّمَ " [...] لَا تُؤَدِّي الْمَرْأَةُ حَقَّ رَبِّهَا حَتَّى تُؤَدِّيَ حَقَّ زَوْجِهَا وَلَوْ سَأَلَهَا نَفْسَهَا وَهِيَ عَلَى قَتَبٍ لَمْ تَمْنَعْهُ " .

The Messenger of Allah (ﷺ) said, "[...] No woman can fulfill her duty to Allah until she has fulfilled her duty to her husband. If he asks her for (intimacy), even if she is sitting on her camel's seat, she must not refuse."

Sunan Ibn Mayah, Hadith number 1853

عَنِ الأَسْوَدِ بْنِ يَزِيدَ، سَأَلْتُ عَائِشَةَ ـ رضى الله عنها ـ " مَا كَانَ النَّبِيُّ صَلَّى اللهُ عَلَيْهِ وَسَلَّمَ يَصْنَعُ فِي الْبَيْتِ " قَالَتْ " كَانَ فِي مِهْنَةِ أَهْلِهِ، فَإِذَا سَمِعَ الأَذَانَ خَرَجَ " .

Narrated Al-Aswad bin Yazid: I asked Aisha, "What did the Prophet (ﷺ) do at home?" She said, "He used to work for his family, and when he heard the adhan (call to prayer), he would go out."

Sahih Al-Bukhari, hadith number 5363

قَالَ رَسُولُ اللهِ صَلَّى اللَّهُ عَلَيْهِ وَسَلَّمَ: " إِنِّي لاَ أَعْلَمُ عَمَلاً أَقْرَبَ إِلَى اللهِ عَزَّ وَجَلَّ مِنْ بِرِّ الْوَالِدَةِ " .

The Messenger of Allah (ﷺ) said, "Indeed, I do not know of any deed that brings a person closer to Allah, the Mighty and Majestic, than kindness and dutifulness to one's mother."

Al Adab Al Mufrad, hadith number 4

HADITHS ON THE
FAMILY AND MARRIED LIFE

قَالَ رَسُولُ اللهِ صَلَّى اللهُ عَلَيْهِ وَسَلَّمَ " كُلُّكُمْ رَاعٍ، وَكُلُّكُمْ مَسْئُولٌ عَنْ
رَعِيَّتِهِ، وَالأَمِيرُ رَاعٍ، وَالرَّجُلُ رَاعٍ عَلَى أَهْلِ بَيْتِهِ، وَالْمَرْأَةُ رَاعِيَةٌ عَلَى
بَيْتِ زَوْجِهَا وَوَلَدِهِ، فَكُلُّكُمْ رَاعٍ وَكُلُّكُمْ مَسْئُولٌ عَنْ رَعِيَّتِهِ ".

The Prophet () said, "Each of you is a shepherd, and
each of you is responsible for their flock. The leader is a
shepherd and is responsible for their subjects. A man is the
shepherd of his household and is responsible for his family.
A woman is the shepherd in the house of her husband
and is responsible for her children. So, each of you is a
shepherd, and each of you is responsible for their flock."

Sahih Al-Bukhari, hadith number 5200

عَنْ عَائِشَةَ قَالَتْ: قَالَ النَّبِيُّ صَلَّى اللهُ عَلَيْهِ وَسَلَّمَ: " إِنَّ أَعْظَمَ النِّكَاحِ بَرَكَةً أَيْسَرُهُ مُؤْنَةً."

Aisha related that the Prophet said, "The marriage that brings
the most blessings is the one that brings the least burdens."

Mishkát al-Masabíh, hadith number 3097

HADITHS ON THE
FAMILY AND MARRIED LIFE

قَالَ النَّبِيُّ صَلَّى اللهُ عَلَيْهِ وَسَلَّمَ " إِذَا أَحَدُكُمْ أَعْجَبَتْهُ الْمَرْأَةُ فَوَقَعَتْ فِي قَلْبِهِ فَلْيَعْمِدْ إِلَى امْرَأَتِهِ فَلْيُوَاقِعْهَا فَإِنَّ ذَلِكَ يَرُدُّ مَا فِي نَفْسِهِ " .

The Prophet (ﷺ) said, "If a woman fascinates one of
you and captivates his heart, he should go to his own
wife and have sexual intercourse with her, for that
will repel his feelings for the other woman."

Sahih Muslim, hadith number 1403 c

كَانَ رَسُولُ اللهِ صَلَّى اللهُ عَلَيْهِ وَسَلَّمَ يُدْرِكُهُ الْفَجْرُ وَهُوَ جُنُبٌ مِنْ أَهْلِهِ، ثُمَّ يَغْتَسِلُ وَيَصُومُ.

The Messenger of Allah (ﷺ) used to bathe and
fast in the morning after having intercourse
with his wives in a state of janaabah.

Sahih Al-Bukhari, hadith number 1925, 1926

قَالَ رَسُولُ اللهِ صَلَّى اللهُ عَلَيْهِ وَسَلَّمَ " لاَ يَفْرَكْ مُؤْمِنٌ مُؤْمِنَةً إِنْ كَرِهَ مِنْهَا خُلُقًا رَضِيَ مِنْهَا آخَرَ " .

The Messenger of Allah (ﷺ) said, "A believing man
should not hate a believing woman. If he dislikes
one of her qualities, he will enjoy another."

Sahih Muslim, hadith number 1468 b

HADITHS ON THE
FAMILY AND MARRIED LIFE

قَالَ النَّبِيُّ صَلَّى اللهُ عَلَيْهِ وَسَلَّمَ " إِذَا اسْتَأْذَنَتِ امْرَأَةُ أَحَدِكُمْ إِلَى الْمَسْجِدِ فَلاَ يَمْنَعْهَا ".

The Prophet (ﷺ) said, "When one of your women seeks
permission to go to the mosque, do not forbid her."

Sahih Al-Bukhari, hadith number 5238

قَالَ رَسُولُ اللهِ صَلَّى اللهُ عَلَيْهِ وَسَلَّمَ " أَكْمَلُ الْمُؤْمِنِينَ إِيمَانًا
أَحْسَنُهُمْ خُلُقًا وَخِيَارُكُمْ خِيَارُكُمْ لِنِسَائِهِمْ خُلُقًا ".

The Messenger of Allah (ﷺ) said, "The most complete
believers in faith are those with the best character, and the
best of you are the best to their women in character."

Yam'a Al Tirmidhi, hadith number 1162

قَالَ رَسُولُ اللهِ صَلَّى اللهُ عَلَيْهِ وَسَلَّمَ " كُلُّ مَعْرُوفٍ صَدَقَةٌ وَإِنَّ مِنَ الْمَعْرُوفِ
أَنْ تَلْقَى أَخَاكَ بِوَجْهٍ طَلْقٍ وَأَنْ تُفْرِغَ مِنْ دَلْوِكَ فِي إِنَاءِ أَخِيكَ ".

The Messenger of Allah(ﷺ) said, "Every act of kindness
is a charity, and among the acts of kindness is to greet
your brother with a cheerful face and to pour water
from your bucket into your brother's container."

Yam'a Al Tirmidhi, hadith number 1970

HADITHS ON THE
FAMILY AND MARRIED LIFE

قَالَ رَسُولُ اللَّهِ صَلَّى اللَّهُ عَلَيْهِ وَسَلَّمَ " إِنَّ اللَّهَ رَفِيقٌ يُحِبُّ الرِّفْقَ وَيُعْطِي عَلَيْهِ مَا لاَ يُعْطِي عَلَى الْعُنْفِ " .

The Messenger of Allah (ﷺ) said, "Allah is kind and loves gentleness, and grants for it a reward which He does not grant for harshness (violence)."

Sunan Ibn Mayah, hadith number 3688

قَالَ رَسُولُ اللَّهِ صَلَّى اللَّهُ عَلَيْهِ وَسَلَّمَ " إِنَّ مِنْ أَكْمَلِ الْمُؤْمِنِينَ إِيمَانًا أَحْسَنُهُمْ خُلُقًا وَأَلْطَفُهُمْ بِأَهْلِهِ " .

The Messenger of Allah (ﷺ) said, "Among the most complete believers in faith are those who are best in character and kindest to their families."

Yam'a Al Tirmidhi, hadith number 2612

عَنْ أَبِي هُرَيْرَةَ، عَنِ النَّبِيِّ صَلَّى اللَّهُ عَلَيْهِ وَسَلَّمَ قَالَ " تُنْكَحُ النِّسَاءُ لِأَرْبَعَةٍ لِمَالِهَا وَلِحَسَبِهَا وَلِجَمَالِهَا وَلِدِينِهَا فَاظْفَرْ بِذَاتِ الدِّينِ تَرِبَتْ يَدَاكَ " .

It was narrated from Abu Huraira that the Prophet (ﷺ) said, "Women marry for four things: their wealth, their lineage, their beauty, and their religious commitment. Choose the one who is religiously committed. Otherwise, you will lose."

Sunan Al-Nasa'i, hadith number 3230

HADITHS ON THE FAMILY AND MARRIED LIFE

نَهَى النَّبِيُّ صَلَّى اللهُ عَلَيْهِ وَسَلَّمَ عَنْ نِكَاحِ الْمُتْعَةِ .

The Messenger of Allah (ﷺ) forbade contracting a temporary marriage.

Sahih Muslim, hadith number 1406 h

قَالَ رَسُولُ اللهِ صَلَّى اللهُ عَلَيْهِ وَسَلَّمَ " لَمْ نَرَ لِلْمُتَحَابَّيْنِ مِثْلَ النِّكَاحِ " .

The Messenger of Allah (ﷺ) said, "There is nothing better than marriage for a man and a woman who love each other."

Sunan Ibn Mayah, hadith number 1847

قَالَ رَسُولُ اللهِ صَلَّى اللهُ عَلَيْهِ وَسَلَّمَ " أَكْرِمُوا أَوْلَادَكُمْ وَأَحْسِنُوا أَدَبَهُمْ " .

The Messenger of Allah (ﷺ) said, "Be kind to your children and perfect their manners."

Sunan Ibn Mayah, hadith number 3671

قَالَ رَسُولُ اللهِ صَلَّى اللهُ عَلَيْهِ وَسَلَّمَ " إِنَّكَ لَنْ تُنْفِقَ نَفَقَةً تَبْتَغِي بِهَا وَجْهَ اللهِ إِلَّا أُجِرْتَ عَلَيْهَا حَتَّى مَا تَجْعَلُ فِي فَمِ امْرَأَتِكَ " .

The Messenger of Allah (ﷺ) said, "Whatever you spend seeking the pleasure of Allah, you will be rewarded for it, even for what you put into the mouth of your wife."

Sahih Al-Bukhari, hadith number 56

HADITHS ON THE
FAMILY AND MARRIED LIFE

قَالَ رَسُولُ اللَّهِ صَلَّى اللَّهُ عَلَيْهِ وَسَلَّمَ " خَيْرُ بَيْتٍ فِي الْمُسْلِمِينَ بَيْتٌ فِيهِ يَتِيمٌ
يُحْسَنُ إِلَيْهِ وَشَرُّ بَيْتٍ فِي الْمُسْلِمِينَ بَيْتٌ فِيهِ يَتِيمٌ يُسَاءُ إِلَيْهِ " .

The Messenger of Allah (ﷺ) said, "The best house among
the Muslims is that in which lives an orphan who is
treated well. And the worst house among the Muslims is
that in which lives an orphan who is treated badly."

Sunan Ibn Mayah, hadith number 3679

سَأَلَ النَّبِيَّ صَلَّى اللَّهُ عَلَيْهِ وَسَلَّمَ " مَا حَقُّ الْمَرْأَةِ عَلَى الزَّوْج قَالَ " أَنْ يُطْعِمَهَا إِذَا طَعِمَ
وَأَنْ يَكْسُوَهَا إِذَا اكْتَسَى وَلاَ يَضْرِبِ الْوَجْهَ وَلاَ يُقَبِّحْ وَلاَ يَهْجُرْ إِلاَّ فِي الْبَيْتِ " .

A man asked the Prophet (ﷺ), "What are the rights of the
wife to her husband?" He replied, "Let him feed her as he
feeds himself, and dress her as he dresses himself; let him
not strike her in the face or disfigure her, and let him not
leave her except in the house (as a form of discipline)."

Sunan Ibn Mayah, Hadith number 1850

قَالَ رَسُولُ اللَّهِ صَلَّى اللَّهُ عَلَيْهِ وَسَلَّمَ " لاَ يَخْطُبِ الرَّجُلُ عَلَى خِطْبَةِ أَخِيهِ " .

The Messenger of Allah (ﷺ) said, "A man should not propose
to a woman to whom his brother has already proposed."

Sunan Ibn Mayah, hadith number 1867

HADITHS ON THE
FAMILY AND MARRIED LIFE

قَالَ رَسُولُ اللهِ صَلَّى اللهُ عَلَيْهِ وَسَلَّمَ " مَنْ حَجَّ لِلهِ فَلَمْ يَرْفُثْ وَلَمْ يَفْسُقْ رَجَعَ كَيَوْمِ وَلَدَتْهُ أُمُّهُ ".

The Prophet (ﷺ) said, "Whoever performs Hajj for the sake of Allah and does not engage in sexual relations or commit sins, he will return like the day his mother gave birth to him."

Sahih Al-Bukhari, hadith number 1521

قَالَ رَسُولُ اللهِ صَلَّى اللهُ عَلَيْهِ وَسَلَّمَ " الْمَرْأَةُ عَوْرَةٌ فَإِذَا خَرَجَتِ اسْتَشْرَفَهَا الشَّيْطَانُ ".

The Prophet (ﷺ) said, "The woman is awra (intimate part of the body to be covered), and when she goes out, the Shaytaan tries to seduce her."

Yam'a Al Tirmidhi, hadith number 1173

قَالَ رَسُولُ اللهِ صَلَّى اللهُ عَلَيْهِ وَسَلَّمَ " بِمَ يَضْرِبُ أَحَدُكُمْ امْرَأَتَهُ ضَرْبَ الْفَحْلِ، ثُمَّ لَعَلَّهُ يُعَانِقُهَا ".

The Prophet (ﷺ) said, "How can any of you beat his wife as one beats the camel's stallion and then he may embrace her (sleep with him)?"

Sahih Al-Bukhari, hadith number 6042

HADITHS ON THE
FAMILY AND MARRIED LIFE

عَنْ جَابِرٍ رَضِيَ اللهُ عَنْهُ قَالَ: قَالَ رَسُولُ اللهِ صَلَّى اللهُ عَلَيْهِ وَسَلَّمَ: "إِلَّا لَا يَبِتن رَجُلٌ عِنْدَ امْرَأَةٍ ثَيِّبٍ إِلَّا أَنْ يَكُونَ ناكحا أَوْ ذَا محرم".

Jabir related that the Messenger of Allah (ﷺ) said, "A man may not spend the night in the house of a married woman unless he is her husband or a close relative."

Mishkát al-Masabíh, hadith number 3101

قَالَ رَسُولُ اللهِ صَلَّى اللهُ عَلَيْهِ وَسَلَّمَ: "إِنَّ مِنْ أَكْبَرِ الْكَبَائِرِ أَنْ يَلْعَنَ الرَّجُلُ وَالِدَيْهِ". قِيلَ يَا رَسُولَ اللهِ وَكَيْفَ يَلْعَنُ الرَّجُلُ وَالِدَيْهِ قَالَ "يَسُبُّ الرَّجُلُ أَبَا الرَّجُلِ، فَيَسُبُّ أَبَاهُ، وَيَسُبُّ أَمَّهُ".

The Messenger of Allah (ﷺ) said. "It is one of the greatest sins for a person to curse his parents." Then he was asked, "O Messenger of Allah, how does a man insult his parents?" The Prophet (ﷺ) replied, "He insults the father of another man, and that man insults his father, and insults his mother."

Sahih Al-Bukhari, hadith number 5973

[...] قَالَ النَّبِيُّ صَلَّى اللهُ عَلَيْهِ وَسَلَّمَ "مَنِ ابْتُلِيَ مِنَ الْبَنَاتِ بِشَيْءٍ فَأَحْسَنَ إِلَيْهِنَّ كُنَّ لَهُ سِتْرًا مِنَ النَّارِ".

[...] The Messenger of Allah (ﷺ) said, "Whoever is blessed with daughters and treats them kindly, they will be a shield for him against the Fire."

Sahih Muslim, hadith number 2629

HADITHS ON THE
FAMILY AND MARRIED LIFE

قَالَ رَسُولُ اللهِ صَلَّى اللَّهُ عَلَيْهِ وَسَلَّمَ " إِذَا أَحَبَّ أَحَدُكُمْ أَخَاهُ فَلْيُعْلِمْهُ إِيَّاهُ " .

The Messenger of Allah (ﷺ) said, "When one of you loves his brother, let him inform him of that."

Sahih Al Tirmidhi, hadith number 2392

قَالَ رَسُولُ اللهِ صَلَّى اللَّهُ عَلَيْهِ وَسَلَّمَ " الْمَرْأَةُ كَالضِّلَعِ، إِنْ أَقَمْتَهَا كَسَرْتَهَا، وَإِنِ اسْتَمْتَعْتَ بِهَا اسْتَمْتَعْتَ بِهَا وَفِيهَا عِوَجٌ ".

The Messenger of Allah (ﷺ) said, "A woman is like a rib; if you try to straighten it, it will break. So, if you want to live happily with her, do not try to straighten her."

Sahih Al-Bukhari, hadith number 5184

قَالَ رَسُولُ اللهِ صَلَّى اللَّهُ عَلَيْهِ وَسَلَّمَ: " أَرْبَعَةُ دَنَانِيرَ: دِينَارًا أَعْطَيْتَهُ مِسْكِينًا، وَدِينَارًا أَعْطَيْتَهُ فِي رَقَبَةٍ، وَدِينَارًا أَنْفَقْتَهُ فِي سَبِيلِ اللهِ، وَدِينَارًا أَنْفَقْتَهُ عَلَى أَهْلِكَ، أَفْضَلُهَا الَّذِي أَنْفَقْتَهُ عَلَى أَهْلِكَ ".

The Messenger of Allah (ﷺ) said, "Four dinars: a dinar that you give to a poor person, a dinar that you give to free a slave, a dinar that you spend for the sake of Allah, and a dinar that you spend on your family. The best of them is the dinar you spend on your family."

Al Adab Al Mufrad, hadith number 751

HADITHS ON THE
FAMILY AND MARRIED LIFE

عَنْ أَسْمَاءَ بِنْتِ أَبِي بَكْرٍ ـ رضى الله عنهما ـ قَالَتْ " قَدِمَتْ عَلَىَّ أُمِّي وَهْىَ مُشْرِكَةٌ، فِي عَهْدِ رَسُولِ اللَّهِ صَلَّى اللَّهُ عَلَيْهِ وَسَلَّمَ، فَاسْتَفْتَيْتُ رَسُولَ اللَّهِ صَلَّى اللَّهُ عَلَيْهِ وَسَلَّمَ قُلْتُ {إِنَّ أُمِّي قَدِمَتْ} وَهْىَ رَاغِبَةٌ، أَفَأَصِلُ أُمِّي قَالَ " نَعَمْ صِلِي أُمَّكِ ".

Asmaa bint Abu Bakr (may Allah be pleased with her)
narrated: "My mother came to me while she was still a
polytheist during the lifetime of the Prophet (ﷺ). I sought the
advice of the Prophet (ﷺ) saying, 'My mother has come to
me and she is asking for my help; should I treat her kindly?'
He replied, 'Yes, keep good relation with your mother.'"

Sahih Al-Bukhari, hadith number 2620

قَالَ رَجُلٌ يَا رَسُولَ اللَّهِ الرَّجُلُ يُحِبُّ الرَّجُلَ عَلَى الْعَمَلِ مِنَ الْخَيْرِ يَعْمَلُ بِهِ وَلاَ يَعْمَلُ بِمِثْلِهِ فَقَالَ رَسُولُ اللَّهِ صَلَّى اللَّهُ عَلَيْهِ وَسَلَّمَ " الْمَرْءُ مَعَ مَنْ أَحَبَّ ".

A man said, "O Messenger of Allah, there are people who
love others for the good deeds they do, but they themselves
cannot do such deeds." The Messenger of Allah (ﷺ) replied
"One will be (in the Hereafter) with those whom he loves."

Sunan Abu Dawûd, hadith number 5127

HADITHS ON THE
FAMILY AND MARRIED LIFE

قَالَ رَسُولُ اللَّهِ صَلَّى اللَّهُ عَلَيْهِ وَسَلَّمَ " اعْدِلُوا بَيْنَ أَبْنَائِكُمْ اعْدِلُوا بَيْنَ أَبْنَائِكُمْ " .

The Messenger of Allah (ﷺ) said, "Be just in treating your
children equally. Be just in treating your children equally."

Sunan Al-Nasa'i, hadith number 3687

قَالَ رَسُولُ اللَّهِ صَلَّى اللَّهُ عَلَيْهِ وَسَلَّمَ " أَبَرُّ الْبِرِّ أَنْ يَصِلَ الرَّجُلُ وُدَّ أَبِيهِ " .

The Messenger of Allah (ﷺ) said, "The most
beautiful act of kindness is when a person treats
his father's relatives with kindness."

Sahih Muslim, hadith number 2552 a

قَالَ رَجُلٌ يَا رَسُولَ اللَّهِ مَنْ أَحَقُّ بِحُسْنِ الصُّحْبَةِ قَالَ " أُمُّكَ
ثُمَّ أُمُّكَ ثُمَّ أُمُّكَ ثُمَّ أَبُوكَ ثُمَّ أَدْنَاكَ أَدْنَاكَ " .

A man asked the Messenger of Allah which of the people
most deserves to be treated well? The Prophet (ﷺ) said:
"Your mother, your mother again, your mother again, then
your father, then your next of kin in order of kinship."

Sahih Muslim, hadith number 2548 b

HADITHS ABOUT PARADISE AND HELL

قَالَ رَسُولُ اللهِ صَلَّى اللهُ عَلَيْهِ وَسَلَّمَ " مَنْ يَضْمَنْ لِي مَا بَيْنَ لَحْيَيْهِ وَمَا بَيْنَ رِجْلَيْهِ أَضْمَنْ لَهُ الْجَنَّةَ ".

The Messenger of Allah (ﷺ) said, "Whoever can guarantee (the chastity) of what is between his jaws (tongue) and between his two legs (his private parts), I guarantee him Paradise."

Sahih Al-Bukhari, hadith number 6474

قَالَ رَسُولُ اللهِ صَلَّى اللهُ عَلَيْهِ وَسَلَّمَ " لاَ يَدْخُلُ الْجَنَّةَ مَنْ كَانَ فِي قَلْبِهِ مِثْقَالُ ذَرَّةٍ مِنْ كِبْرٍ " .

The Messenger of Allah (ﷺ) said, "He will not enter Paradise who has in his heart the weight of a mustard seed of arrogance."

Sahih Muslim, hadith number 91 c

قَالَ رَسُولُ اللهِ صَلَّى اللهُ عَلَيْهِ وَسَلَّمَ "من أحبَّ أن يُزحزحَ عن النار، ويدخلَ الجنةَ، فلتأتِه منيته وهو يؤمنُ باللهِ واليومِ الآخرِ، وليأتِ إلى الناسِ الذي يحبُّ أن يؤتى إليه".

The Messenger of Allah (ﷺ) said, "Whoever loves to be removed from the Hellfire and admitted to Paradise should die with faith in Allah and the Last Day, and should treat people as he wishes to be treated."

Riyad as-Salihin, hadith number 1566

HADITHS ABOUT
PARADISE AND HELL

قَالَ رَسُولُ اللهِ صَلَّى اللهُ عَلَيْهِ وَسَلَّمَ " أَيُّمَا امْرَأَةٍ مَاتَتْ وَزَوْجُهَا عَنْهَا رَاضٍ دَخَلَتِ الْجَنَّةَ " .

The Messenger of Allah (ﷺ) said, "Every woman who dies
when her husband is satisfied with her will enter Paradise."

Sunan Ibn Mayah, Hadith number 1854

قَالَ رَسُولُ اللهِ صَلَّى اللهُ عَلَيْهِ وَسَلَّمَ " أَفْضَلُ الْجِهَادِ كَلِمَةُ عَدْلٍ عِنْدَ سُلْطَانٍ جَائِرٍ " .

The Prophet (ﷺ) said, "The best form of jihad is to speak
a word of truth in the presence of a tyrannical ruler."

Sunan Abu Dawūd, hadith number 4344

كنا عند رسولِ اللهِ صَلَّى اللهُ عَلَيْهِ وَسَلَّمَ فنظرَ إلى القمرِ ليلةَ البدرِ، وقَالَ:
"إنكم سَترونَ ربَّكم عياناً كما تَرونَ هذا القمرَ، لا تضامون في رؤيته " .

We were sitting with the Messenger of Allah (ﷺ) when he
looked at the full moon and said, "You will see your Lord
in the Hereafter as you see this moon, and you will not
feel the slightest discomfort when you look at Him."

Riyad as-Salihin, Hadith number 1895

HADITHS ABOUT PARADISE AND HELL

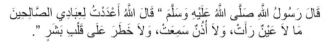

قَالَ رَسُولُ اللهِ صَلَّى اللهُ عَلَيْهِ وَسَلَّمَ " قَالَ اللهُ أَعْدَدْتُ لِعِبَادِي الصَّالِحِينَ مَا لاَ عَيْنٌ رَأَتْ، وَلاَ أُذُنٌ سَمِعَتْ، وَلاَ خَطَرَ عَلَى قَلْبِ بَشَرٍ ".

The Prophet (ﷺ) said, "Allah said, I have prepared for My righteous servants what no eye has seen, no ear has heard, and it has never occurred to the human heart."

Sahih Al-Bukhari, hadith number 7498

قَالَ رَسُولُ اللهِ صَلَّى اللهُ عَلَيْهِ وَسَلَّمَ " مَنْ سَلَكَ طَرِيقًا يَلْتَمِسُ فِيهِ عِلْمًا سَهَّلَ اللهُ لَهُ طَرِيقًا إِلَى الْجَنَّةِ ".

The Messenger of Allah (ﷺ) said, "Whoever undertakes a path to attain knowledge, Allah makes the way to Paradise easy for him."

Yam'a Al Tirmidhi, hadith number 2646

قَالَ رَسُولُ اللهِ صَلَّى اللهُ عَلَيْهِ وَسَلَّمَ " لاَ تَدْخُلُونَ الْجَنَّةَ حَتَّى تُؤْمِنُوا وَلاَ تُؤْمِنُوا حَتَّى تَحَابُّوا . أَوَلاَ أَدُلُّكُمْ عَلَى شَيْءٍ إِذَا فَعَلْتُمُوهُ تَحَابَبْتُمْ أَفْشُوا السَّلاَمَ بَيْنَكُمْ " .

The Messenger of Allah (ﷺ) said, "You will not enter Paradise until you believe, and you will not believe until you love each other. Shall I show you something that, if you did, you would love each other? Spread peace among yourselves."

Sahih Muslim, hadith number 54 a

HADITHS ABOUT PARADISE AND HELL

قَالَ رَسُولُ اللَّهِ صَلَّى اللَّهُ عَلَيْهِ وَسَلَّمَ " مَا أَمَرْتُكُمْ بِهِ فَخُذُوهُ وَمَا نَهَيْتُكُمْ عَنْهُ فَانْتَهُوا ".

The Prophet (ﷺ) said, "Whatever I have commanded you, do it, and whatever I have forbidden you, abstain from it."

Sunan Ibn Mayah, Hadith number 1

قَالَ رَسُولُ اللَّهِ صَلَّى اللَّهُ عَلَيْهِ وَسَلَّمَ " حُجِبَتِ النَّارُ بِالشَّهَوَاتِ، وَحُجِبَتِ الْجَنَّةُ بِالْمَكَارِهِ ".

The Messenger of Allah (ﷺ) said, "The Hellfire is surrounded by all kinds of desires and passions, while Paradise is surrounded by all kinds of unlovable and undesirable things."

Sahih Al-Bukhari, hadith number 6487

قَالَ رَسُولُ اللَّهِ صَلَّى اللَّهُ عَلَيْهِ وَسَلَّمَ " يَقُولُ اللَّهُ تَعَالَى مَا لِعَبْدِي الْمُؤْمِنِ عِنْدِي جَزَاءٌ، إِذَا قَبَضْتُ صَفِيَّهُ مِنْ أَهْلِ الدُّنْيَا، ثُمَّ احْتَسَبَهُ إِلاَّ الْجَنَّةُ ".

The Messenger of Allah (ﷺ) said, "Allah says, ‹I have nothing but Paradise as a reward for My believing servant who, if I let his dear friend (or relative) die, remains patient (and awaits Allah's reward).›"

Sahih Al-Bukhari, hadith number 6424

HADITHS ABOUT PARADISE AND HELL

قَالَ رَسُولُ اللَّهِ صَلَّى اللَّهُ عَلَيْهِ وَسَلَّمَ " سَبْعَةٌ يُظِلُّهُمُ اللَّهُ، رَجُلٌ ذَكَرَ اللَّهَ فَفَاضَتْ عَيْنَاهُ ".

The Prophet (ﷺ) said, "Allah will shelter seven (types of people) under His shadow (on the Day of Resurrection): (One of them will be) a person who sheds tears at the thought of Allah."

Sahih Al-Bukhari, hadith number 6479

قال النبي صَلَّى اللَّهُ عَلَيْهِ وَسَلَّمَ " الجنَّةُ أقربُ إلى أحدِكمْ مِنْ شِراكِ نَعْلِيهِ، والنَّارُ كذلك ".

The Prophet (ﷺ) said, "Paradise is nearer than a shoelace to each of you, and so is the Fire of Hell."

Riyad as-Salihin, hadith number 105

قال النبي صَلَّى اللَّهُ عَلَيْهِ وَسَلَّمَ " إِنَّ لِلَّهِ تِسْعَةً وَتِسْعِينَ اسْمًا مَنْ أَحْصَاهَا دَخَلَ الْجَنَّةَ ".

The Prophet (ﷺ) said, "Allah has ninety-nine names; whoever learns them will enter Paradise."

Sahih Al Tirmidhi, hadith number 3508

HADITHS ABOUT PARADISE AND HELL

سَمِعْتُ رَسُولَ اللَّهِ صَلَّى اللَّهُ عَلَيْهِ وَسَلَّمَ يَقُولُ " مَنْ بَنَى مَسْجِدًا لِلَّهِ بَنَى اللَّهُ لَهُ فِي الْجَنَّةِ مِثْلَهُ ".

I heard Allah's Messenger (ﷺ) say, "Whoever builds a mosque for Allah, Allah will build him in Paradise a similar house."

Sahih Muslim, hadith number 533 d

قَالَ رَسُولُ اللَّهِ صَلَّى اللَّهُ عَلَيْهِ وَسَلَّمَ: " كلُّ أُمَّتِي يَدخلونَ الجنَّةَ إلا مَنْ أبَى " . قِيل: ومَنْ يأْبى يا رسول اللهِ قَالَ: " مَنْ أطَاعني دخلَ الجنَّةَ ومَنْ عصَاني فقد أبَى".

The Messenger of Allah (ﷺ) said, "All those of my Ummah (community of faith) will enter Paradise except those who refuse." They asked him, "Who will refuse?" He (ﷺ) said, "Whoever obeys me will enter Paradise, and whoever disobeys me will refuse to enter Paradise."

Riyad as-Salihin, hadith number 158

قَالَ رَسُولُ اللَّهِ صَلَّى اللَّهُ عَلَيْهِ وَسَلَّمَ " مَا مِنْ مُسْلِمٍ يُتَوَفَّى لَهُ ثَلاَثَةٌ مِنَ الْوَلَدِ لَمْ يَبْلُغُوا الْحِنْثَ إِلاَّ أَدْخَلَهُ اللَّهُ الْجَنَّةَ بِفَضْلِ رَحْمَتِهِ إِيَّاهُمْ " .

The Messenger of Allah (ﷺ) said, "Any Muslim whose three children die before reaching the age of puberty will be granted Paradise by Allah out of His mercy towards them."

Sunan Al-Nasa'i, hadith number 1873

HADITHS ABOUT PARADISE AND HELL

قَالَ رَسُولُ اللهِ صَلَّى اللهُ عَلَيْهِ وَسَلَّمَ " قَالَ اللهُ عَزَّ وَجَلَّ الْمُتَحَابُّونَ فِي جَلَالِي لَهُمْ مَنَابِرُ مِنْ نُورٍ يَغْبِطُهُمُ النَّبِيُّونَ وَالشُّهَدَاءُ " .

The Messenger of Allah (ﷺ) said, "Allah, the Mighty and Exalted, said: Those who love each other for the sake of My Majesty will stand on pedestals of light and will be admired by the prophets and the martyrs.'"

Yam'a Al Tirmidhi, hadith number 2390

قَالَ رَسُولُ اللهِ صَلَّى اللهُ عَلَيْهِ وَسَلَّمَ: " إِنَّ الصِّدْقَ يَهْدِي إِلَى الْبِرِّ ، وَإِنَّ الْبِرَّ يَهْدِي إِلَى الْجَنَّةِ ، وَإِنَّ الرَّجُلَ لَيَصْدُقُ حَتَّى يَكُونَ صِدِّيقًا. وَإِنَّ الْكَذِبَ يَهْدِي إِلَى الْفُجُورِ ، وَإِنَّ الْفُجُورَ يَهْدِي إِلَى النَّارِ ، وَإِنَّ الرَّجُلَ لَيَكْذِبُ حَتَّى يُكْتَبَ عِنْدَ اللهِ كَذَّابًا " .

The Messenger of Allah (ﷺ) said, "Verily, truthfulness leads to righteousness and righteousness leads to Paradise. A man continues to speak the truth until he is written with Allah as a truthful person. Falsehood leads to wickedness and wickedness leads to the Hellfire. A man continues to tell lies until he is written with Allah as a liar."

Sahih Muslim, hadith number 2607 b

قَالَ رَسُولُ اللهِ صَلَّى اللهُ عَلَيْهِ وَسَلَّمَ " يَقُولُ اللهُ عَزَّ وَجَلَّ مَنْ أَذْهَبْتُ حَبِيبَتَيْهِ فَصَبَرَ وَاحْتَسَبَ لَمْ أَرْضَ لَهُ ثَوَابًا دُونَ الْجَنَّةِ " .

The Messenger of Allah (ﷺ) said, "Allah, Mighty and Exalted, said, 'Whosoever takes his sight from Him and is patient and seeks a reward, for him I want no less reward than Paradise.'"

Sahih Al Tirmidhi, hadith number 2401

HADITHS ABOUT PARADISE AND HELL

قَالَ رَسُولُ اللَّهِ صَلَّى اللَّهُ عَلَيْهِ وَسَلَّمَ " أَنَا زَعِيمٌ بِبَيْتٍ فِي رَبَضِ الْجَنَّةِ
لِمَنْ تَرَكَ الْمِرَاءَ وَإِنْ كَانَ مُحِقًّا وَبِبَيْتٍ فِي وَسَطِ الْجَنَّةِ لِمَنْ تَرَكَ الْكَذِبَ
وَإِنْ كَانَ مَازِحًا وَبِبَيْتٍ فِي أَعْلَى الْجَنَّةِ لِمَنْ حَسَّنَ خُلُقَهُ " .

The Prophet (ﷺ) said, "I guarantee a house in the neighborhood
of Paradise for a man who avoids arguing even if he is
right. A house in the center of Paradise for a man who
avoids lying even if he is joking, and a house in the upper
part of Paradise for a man who has a good character."

Sunan Abu Dawûd, hadith number 4800

EPILOGUE

You have reached the end of this book and we hope you have enjoyed reading it and have been inspired by the wisdom of our Prophet Muhammad (ﷺ). We will be delighted if this book has given you new strength, broadened your knowledge of Islam and deepened your relationship with Allah (ﷻ).

But the use of this book should not end here! Check out the book more often, read the wise words of the Prophet Muhammad (ﷺ) and let them guide and inspire you in your daily life. The Prophet's teachings are timeless and offer valuable insights for various life situations. By regularly studying and reflecting on these words, you can not only deepen your understanding of the Islamic faith, but also find practical wisdom and spiritual guidance for your personal growth and daily challenges.

If you liked this book and want to spread the message of Islam, please feel free to recommend it to others.

بارك الله فيك

(May Allah bless you)
Ibrahim Al-Abadi and Islam Way

Printed in Great Britain
by Amazon

44856506R00076